T0078399

MIRACLES, SIGNS AND WONDERS

DIANNE CHATMAN

WESTBOW
PRESS®
A DIVISION OF THOMAS NELSON
& ZONDERVAN

WestBow Press books may be ordered through booksellers or by contacting:

WestBow Press
A Division of Thomas Nelson & Zondervan
1663 Liberty Drive
Bloomington, IN 47403
www.westbowpress.com
844-714-3454

Scripture quotations marked KJV are taken from the King James Version.

Scripture quotations marked NIV are taken from The Holy Bible, New
International Version®, NIV® Copyright © 1973, 1978, 1984, 2011 by
Biblica, Inc.® Used by permission. All rights reserved worldwide.

ISBN: 978-1-6642-1583-2 (sc)
ISBN: 978-1-6642-1584-9 (hc)
ISBN: 978-1-6642-1582-5 (e)

Library of Congress Control Number: 2020924583

Print information available on the last page.

WestBow Press rev. date: 12/10/2020

INTRODUCTION

We live in a world that **is** both spiritual and natural we ourselves are a spirit living in a natural body which also possesses a soul (**1 Thessalonians 5: 23, KJV**). As God breathed a living soul and a spirit into a body formed out of the dust of the earth, the 6th day of creation, and man came into being (Genesis 2:7), because of that, at the moment of conception we are also given a living soul and a spirit by God the Father of all creation. We are a tri- part being; we are body, soul and spirit, just like the Godhead: Father, Son, and Holy Ghost, are three but touching and agreeing as one. Now when we are born again of the Spirit and Jesus Christ becomes Lord and Savior over our lives, our spirit, which was once dormant, (inactive) without Christ, is quickened, made alive, through the Holy Spirit, (**John 6: 63, KJV),** or awakened out of its dormant state, and thus we are born again of the Spirit, and when we receive the Baptism of the Holy Ghost, we become "the new man", born again. Thus bringing to light, (understanding), and life, recognition of our spiritual side, whereas we begin to see as we never saw before, hear as we never heard before, understand as we never understood before through the power and the workings of the Holy Ghost which we receive through the Baptism of the Holy Ghost experience. Why you may ask the importance of making such statements? Because without the spirit of Christ dwelling within us to open our eyes to the truth of what has taken place, often we miss or do not recognize the working of miracles, signs and wonders of God that He does in our lives, (**Romans 8:5, KJV**), we try to explain it off as an unexplainable phenomenon, unwilling to accept the truth at times that there is a true and living God, all powerful, all knowing, and all present, at all times in our lives. This is why we need Jesus in our lives and at the head of our lives and the guidance of the indwelling Holy Spirit, so that our eyes can be made open unto the spirit and the truth that is around us, (**John 10: 10, KJV**). Without Christ to activate or make alive our spirit within us there remains an unawareness of the things of the spirit and the life of the spirit that is living and moving and active all around us every day. The graciousness, the mercy, the love and unwarranted favor of God will not be truly recognized or valued for what it is, a gift from God. It would just be considered as one of those in-explainable events or coincidences. God through Jesus Christ and the power of the Holy Ghost, is still doing wonderful and mighty miracles all around the world for His people, and trying to bring us into a closer relationship with Him and giving us just a glimpse of who He is and what He can do for His people if we would just turn to Him in love, believing in Him and trusting Him, seeking to walk in His ways, the ways of love. I have had the blessing of experiencing many miracles in my life, times when I really needed them and needed to know that God was there and He has never failed me. Because I trusted Him and took Him at His word and tried my best to live according to His word, I am not saying I was successful always. I have had my down moments when I did not listen and have had to reap the consequences of my own actions, but even in these, God was still merciful and gracious to forgive me and help me to get back up again. That's the kind of God we serve. He is a loving, longsuffering, patient and kind Father, but we need to know, He is a Father and that being said, we are expected to live according to His will. After all, heaven is His throne and earth is His footstool, **(Isaiah 66:1, KJV)**. It is my prayer that they will inspire you to believe He is creator of heaven and earth, **(Genesis 1:1, KJV)**. He is the God of the impossible, and if you do not have a relationship with Him already, now is the time to seek to be in relationship with Him through Jesus Christ our Lord and Savior. As we see time wrapping up and the prophecies of the end times manifesting all around us from day to day, we know that time draws nearer, even at the door to Christ's coming, let us seek to know Him better by drawing nearer to God in the spirit, truly the passage in 1 Corinthians says it all. –

"But as it is written, Eye hath not seen nor ear heard, neither have entered into the heart of man, the things which God hath prepared for them that love Him." -(

DEDICATIONS

To the Body of Christ and to those who would seek to know Jesus as their Lord and Savior and to be joined unto Him, that you will know, we serve an all powerful God who is also a loving Father, and Jesus Christ who loves us beyond words and means, who sent to us the Holy Spirit to come and dwell within us to reveal to us great and mighty things, and who also empowers us to do great things in Jesus name, we receive great things from God our Father, the Father of lights.

Every good gift and every perfect gift is from above, and cometh down from the Father of lights, with whom is no variableness, neither shadow of turning." – (James 1:17, KJV)

"A man that hath friends must first shew himself friendly: and there is a friend that sticketh closer than a brother. - (Proverbs 18: 24, KJV)

For My Friends

A Day of Sunshine

And there they preached the gospel.

And there sat a certain man at Lystra, impotent in his feet, being a cripple from his mother's womb, who never had walked:

The same heard Paul speak: who stedfastly beholding him, and perceiving that he had faith to be healed,

Said with a loud voice, Stand upright on thy feet. And he leaped and walked. – (Acts 14: 8 - 10, KJV)

This man's day of sunshine came when he had faith to believe that he could be healed. Listening to Paul and Barnabas preaching and giving testimony unto Jesus Christ, he took hold of faith. Paul shouted to him to stand upright on his feet. The lame man heard Paul calling for him to stand up, he stood up. Oh what a joyful day to be loosed from a bondage that had one crippled from birth! I can only imagine the joy this man must have felt, to be able for the first time in his life to stand up on his own two feet without having to be carried everywhere he went, all because he listened and received in his heart the word of testimony which was spoken by Paul and Barnabas concerning Jesus Christ. The word of God tells us that - Faith cometh by hearing and hearing by the word of God, - (Romans 10:17, KJV). It is what the lame man heard about Jesus that encouraged him to have faith in the name of Jesus and to believe for his healing, and by doing so, he was healed. All throughout the Bible we are encouraged to hear what the Lord is saying, had not the lame man been listening, hearing, and receiving the word that was spoken, he would have missed his healing! There is power in the word of God and that power is transferred when we believe and receive the word in our hearts!

He that hath ears to hear, let him hear – (Matthew 11: 15, KJV)

✦ TESTIMONIES OF THE HEART:

Back in 1994 in the snowy month of January, I was getting ready to go to Wednesday night Bible Study. Hearing the horn blow outside of church members who had come to pick me up for Bible study, I slipped on some ice that had been covered over by fresh fallen snow as I was hurrying down the steps outside my house. Being that it was night and it was somewhat dark outside, I stepped on a patch of ice. Because it was covered over by a thin layer of snow that had accumulated on top of it, I did not see it. My foot immediately slipped and shot out from under me, twisted all the way around and snapped. I lost my balance and started falling head first forward and down the rest of the steps towards the icy cold cement that made up my walkway. I quickly called out, JESUS!!! Immediately, it felt like two arms just picked up my body and threw me over the railing to the right and into the pile of snow at the bottom of the steps on the right side of the walkway! My legs and feet were sticking out of the pile of snow and my left foot that had snapped was flopping around my leg like a rag doll! Some of the ones in the car asked me after helping me get to the car and in it, how did I go up in the air and over the railing the way that I did? I could not answer that, because I didn't know myself, except Jesus! Hoping that it was just a sprain, I went to church anyway, I received prayer and anointing oil was poured on my leg which ran down into my boot, because my ankle and leg had become very swollen. I hopped around on my right foot all that night and the next day, still hoping that it was just a sprain. I still couldn't put the left foot down without it flopping over onto the side of my leg, still not wanting to accept that anything else was wrong. A member of the church came over the next day to see about me. Watching me hop around on my right foot and falling when I accidentally put my left foot down, immediately exclaimed that she was taking me to the hospital and she was not taking no for an answer, thank God! I found out later after surgery that I had not only had broken a bone, but I had completely torn my left foot from my leg on the inside they said my foot was hanging by one thin bone and that was all. It required several screws and nails in my foot and ankle and a titanium metal plate up my leg, nine hours of surgery and a big thick and heavy cast to hold my foot to my leg and a wheelchair. Needless to say I was told I would never be able to bear weight on my leg and foot again and I would always need a wheel chair for the rest of my life. In others words I couldn't walk. But God! Several months later my pastor, who is now deceased, and in the arms of Jesus God bless him, sent for me to come up to the altar. I rolled my wheelchair up to the altar feeling very discouraged. When I got there, he told me that the Lord had told him that I would be walking in three days. I heard him, but to be honest, I smiled and thanked him for the word, but I had become so discouraged that I wasn't fully persuaded yet at the time. I told myself that he was just feeling sorry for me. That was on a Sunday. That Wednesday three days later as my pastor said the Lord had told him, I was sitting on the side of my bed wondering how I was going to get back downstairs and thinking that I was going to be stuck up stairs until my son came home. Because I wanted to go to the bathroom, I had pulled myself up backwards upstairs to get to the bathroom. I was tired of the potty chair downstairs which sat beside the hospital bed in my living room. Yeah, it was that bad. When the injury happened, I was already dealing with a sickness s I was told that I would have till I died which unfortunately made matters worse. Once again, but God! I sat there trying to figure out how I would attempt to somehow get myself back downstairs. My bedroom sat across the hall from the bathroom. Looking at the door of my bedroom, I wondered what it would feel like to sleep in my own bed. I pulled myself across the floor because my right was too weak for me to stand up on, so I crawled. Having reached the door, I opened it and crawled to the floor to the foot of the bed. Pulling myself up, I sat on the end of the bed, it felt so good. It was then I heard the voice of the Lord speak to me asking me, "Do you want to walk?" Surprised, I immediately said, "Yes Lord, I want to walk." He told me to pull myself up by the door and stand up. My closet sat right at the bottom of my bed to the right. I grabbed hold unto the door frame and started pulling myself up. Extreme pain shot down both of my legs! It was more than I could stand. I sat back down. Disappointed that it was so painful, I started to get discouraged. Again I heard the voice of the Lord speaking to me, asking me, "Do you want to walk?" I answered, and said, Lord, it's too painful. I heard the Spirit of the Lord say," Look up". When I looked up He told me to look at the wall. While I was looking, I had a vision. I saw the doctor telling my guardian, who was also my pastor at the time, because I had no one else, that in two months I would be dead in that wheelchair. He had called him to come into his office that he wanted to talk to him concerning me. I knew the vision was true because I could feel my heart growing weaker and weaker by the day the longer I sat in that wheelchair. Again I heard the voice of the Lord speaking to me. He said, "If you do not get out of the chair, you are going to die in the chair." He told me again to "Stand up". He told me that it would hurt at first, but then the pain would go away." He told me that He would strengthen my legs to hold me up." Thinking about how I didn't want to die in the wheelchair, I reached out once again to pull myself up by the door frame of my closet. Yes, it hurt, but I took faith in what the Lord had said to me, and immediately it felt like two steel bars went down both of my legs on the inside! Standing up, not feeling any of the weakness

I had felt earlier, but the strength that was now coming from the feeling of iron bars in my legs. I walked out of my bedroom and down the stairs to my living room! And yes, the pain did subside as the Lord said it would. Once again, I heard the voice of the Lord telling me to have the medical supply place to come and take their equipment back, that I no longer needed it. Excited and happy, I quickly called the medical supply place and told them that they could come and pick up the equipment. The receptionist that answered the phone was surprised. She wanted to know what had happened that I no longer needed the equipment. Had my doctor got in touch with me, and said that I no longer need the wheelchair. I told her no, but that God had healed me and I was walking! and to call and to tell them that they could come and pick up their equipment, I no longer needed them. She asked me if I was sure about that I told her yes. She told me someone would be right out to pick up the equipment. I guess they just wanted to see me for themselves, because they would usually tell you that they would be out in a day or two. An hour later the driver of the medical supply place was knocking on the door. When he came in he just kind of stood in the middle of the floor and stared at me. He said that when he got the message to come out right away and pick up the equipment, he was surprised because they were told I would have the chair along time until I needed a another one. I asked him if he was going to need any help getting the equipment out the door. He looked at me, shook his head and put a hand on his hip and said, "You are actually walking!" While laughing at the same time, He went on to say no I got it!" I found myself laughing as well at my boldness to ask him if he needed help. I have been walking ever since.

That evening when the pastor saw me walking, in his amazement he shared with me how that the doctor had called him into his office to talk to him. Before he could finish telling me what he said, I shared with him the vision the Lord had given me earlier and how He healed me and got me out of the wheelchair so I could walk again. He told me how that I was right. When I went back to have my cast removed and everyone saw me walking instead of riding in a wheelchair, knowing the type of injury I had sustained from slipping and falling because of the ice and what my outcome was supposed to had been, they started calling me the miracle woman. All this because I heard the Lord, and the word from the Lord and took faith in what in He said, I received my healing and I am walking today and that was 26 years ago and counting! Its' funny how the Lord does things, those little but monumental things that we sometimes overlook that bears His signature on them, those things that standout that tells others as well as one's self, that surely this was the hand of the Lord.

This particular miracle brings to my min the scripture found in - Psalm 118: 23, (KJV);

This is the LORD's doing; it is marvelous in our eyes. - **(Psalm 118:23, KJV)**

The injury happened on a Wednesday on the way to Bible study, here again, it was another Wednesday and I was once again, on my way to another Bible study. This time though, I was healed and walking! God does have a sense of humor! That day the Lord did shine ever so brightly in my life. It truly was a day of sunshine for me. God turned what could have been a very dark time for me into something so bright and beautiful until every time I think about, it makes me laugh with joy in the Lord!

Bless ye the LORD, all ye servants of the LORD, which by night stand in the house of the LORD.

Lift up your hands in the sanctuary and bless the LORD. – (Psalm 134:1, 2, KJV)

THE BARREL OF MEAL

And she said, As the Lord thy God liveth, I have not cake, but an handful of meal in a barrel, and a little oil in a cruse: and, behold, I am gathering two sticks, that I may go in and dress it for me and my son, that we may eat it, and die.

And Elijah said unto her, fear not; go and do as thou hast said: but make me thereof a little cake first, and bring it unto me, and after make for thee and for thy son.

For thus saith the Lord God of Israel, The barrel of meal shall not waste, neither shall the cruse of oil fail, until the day that the LORD sendeth rain upon the earth. – (1 King 17: 12 – 14, KJV)

Sometimes in life we run into times when we just don't have enough to make it. Those times when we are in between barely enough and not enough and it looks like there is no one to help us and on top of that, there's someone else to take care, but for the love of Jesus. This widow didn't have anything she was fixing her last meal for her and her son to eat and die. There was a drought in the land and no rain, so nothing was growing. The prophet Elijah the man of God, came to the woman to ask her for a cake of bread made of the woman's last bit of meal that she had in a barrel. She could have said no, I don't have enough you are going to have to go somewhere else, but, by doing so, she would have missed her miracle. Opening up her heart to share of what she had in a time when she herself didn't have enough to share, caused God bless her barrel of meal not to run out until the rains came. The rains meant that the wheat and the grain harvest would grow and there would be enough for everybody to enjoy. These are times when you don't have enough that when you trust God and stretch out on your faith, God answers. Not only did her barrel not run out of meal, but the cruse of oil that she had left did not run out either! Not to mention that when her son became sick and died God working through the prophet Elijah brought him back to life! ;

And he cried unto the LORD, and said, O LORD my God, hast Thou also brought evil upon the widow with whom I sojourn, by slaying her son?

And he stretched himself upon the child three times, and cried unto the LORD, and said, O LORD my God, I pray Thee, let this child's soul come into him again.

And the LORD heard the voice of Elijah; and the soul of the child came into him again, and he revived. – 1 Kings 17: 21- 22, (KJV)

Two miracles, the second even all the more greater than the first, what a blessing! All because she stretched her faith to include the man of God in her last meal and share with him her last bit of meal that she was going to use to make one last cake of bread for her and her son to eat and then to die. Believing the prophet Elijah and what he said God would do baked the cake. Just as the man of God told her, she received double for her trouble! Meal to last the entire time of the drought so that all who were in the house would not starve and her only son brought back to life! This was a bright and sunny day for the widow and her house!

→ Testimonies of the Heart:

I remember in the summer of 1981, I had my own kind of "drought" going on. I was running out of food and I didn't have enough to make a complete meal daily to feed my children. I was also feeding a neighbor and her child at same time. They were going through just as much of a tough time as I and my children and much of the time didn't have any food to eat at all. I took it upon myself to make sure that they had a meal to eat everyday along with me and my children. Every time I cooked a meal for me and my children I would invite them over to join us. I knew she was feeling too embarrassed to ask, so I took it upon myself to ask her. I knew what she was going through and didn't want to embarrass her and since her child played every day with my children, I made it look like I just couldn't see him go home hungry after playing with my children all day. In turn it allowed me to invite her as well. I was glad when she accepted my offer. I knew her and her child would go home with a full stomach. I kept her child all day until she came home and fed him right along with mine, breakfast lunch and dinner when I would invite her as well. One time I didn't have enough to stretch the meals until I could buy more food. My son and my daughter both liked my cornbread because I would make it sweet and the neighbor's child did too. I knew if I could make a pan of cornbread a day it would help stretch the meal and I would have enough for us to eat and be full until I could get more.

In my Bible studies, I had read the passage in - 1 King 17: 8- 16, (KJV), about God stretching a widow woman's meal in the barrel after she baked a cake of bread for the prophet Elijah to eat and she did. I took faith that if I prayed and asked the Lord to do the same miracle for me and stretch the cornmeal that I had in my canister so that I could continue to preparing full meals for me and my neighbor until I could get more food that maybe He would bless me and answer my request. I started praying. I first reminded the Lord what He said in His word;

For I am the LORD, I change not: - (Malachi 3:6, KJV)

Jesus Christ the same yesterday, and to day, and for ever – (Hebrews 13:8, KJV)

I said, Lord if you change not and you are the same yesterday, today and forever, then that means, what you did back then you can do it again. I asked Him to please do for me what He did for the widow in the Bible and bless the cornmeal I had in the canister to stretch until I could buy some more. Emboldened my circumstance I stretched out on faith and challenged the Lord to consider me as He considered the widow and her son, when she had not enough, but was willing to feed someone else along with her and her son, even though she knew it was her last. She stretched out on faith and believed the prophet and fed him first. I know this sounds like I was pushing it, but desperate times called for desperate measures. I needed the Lord's supernatural help and I knew if He did it once for someone else in need, and He is a God that does not change, He could do it again for me and I felt no shame in asking Him to please, do it again.

I had exactly one and a third cup of cornmeal left in the canister. Every day for five days straight I would take out exactly one cup of cornmeal which left one third cup of cornmeal in the canister. Every day for five days straight I would ask my neighbor to measure what was left in the canister for a witness. The first two days they insisted that I had some cornmeal put up somewhere in the apartment and had to be putting the cornmeal back in the can myself. Each time, for their own assurance that I was not doing this, I would let them search my apartment by their self. I had a one bedroom apartment that wasn't very big, so it was no big deal to let them do this. I wanted a witness myself. In fact I thought it was kind of funny, I had nothing to hide. When they would get through, I would just smile at them and ask them if they were finished? My neighbor walked back over toward me with this bewildered look on her face and would just stand there and stare at me while putting one hand on her hip. Knowing what God was doing, I did not want to share this miracle alone. I was determined to prove God was not just the God of the Bible, but the God of this whole world and creator of all things today and what He did yesterday He could do it again today. I had put God to the test, and He did not fail me, and to my necessity I had no other choice, I desperately needed His help. Each day I would have exactly one third cup of cornmeal left in the canister after I would have taken exactly one cup to make cornbread for us to eat with our meal! To my neighbor's astonishment and to my marvel at the supernatural work of God, each day I would open the canister to take out the meal, it looked like there was only a cup left in the canister. I would get my measuring cup and dip into the canister to measure out a cup of cornmeal thinking that surely this was going to take all the cornmeal left in the canister. After I would have taken out the cup thinking that it was all, the meal seemed to multiply at the bottom of the canister to amount of one third cup, exactly! I would have scooped it out, and it looked to be all but gone, just to watch it stretch back out across the bottom of the canister! I called my neighbor over to see this miracle for their selves. On the third and fourth day since they thought that it was me putting the meal back into the canister the first two days I had them to come over and measure what was left in the canister. The two of us would stare in wonder and amazement at the bottom of the canister every time the meal stretched across the bottom of the canister after all but being emptied out. It was simply amazing to watch to say the least! I believe because I was willing to share what I had with my neighbor, out of my own necessity, gave me the courage to put my God to the test, in faith, that what He did for another, He would be willing to do for me. This also was a test of my faith as well, in asking God for a Bible miracle was a test of what I was willing to believe God for as well, and as I stated earlier He did not let me down. God did it and He did it before me and my neighbor's eyes. What a wonderful God we serve! He is not afraid of confrontation, He doesn't back down when challenged, nor does He hesitate when He is asked to step in on our behalf. God is well able to meet any challenge head on, proving that He is more than able. He is not just God, He is God Almighty! That was my miracle of the meal in the barrel. I claimed it in the name of Jesus and God provided it for me and my children until I got paid at the end of the week, exactly five days later! I knew I still wanted to provide something to eat not just for my children, but I still was concerned about my neighbor as well. I wanted them to have a meal to eat as well along with me and children and God provided, He provided for both of our families, to God be the Glory! These miracles and more are just some of the reasons why I love Christ so, if He had not come into my life, where would I be?

Prove me now herewith, saith the LORD of hosts, if I will not open you the windows of heaven, and pour you out a blessing, that there shall not be room enough to receive it." – (Malachi 3: 10, KJV)

THE WINTER GLOVES

For everyone that asketh receiveth; and he that seeketh findeth; and to him that knocketh it shall be opened.

Or what man is there of you, whom if his son ask bread, will he give him a stone?

Or if he ask a fish, will he give him a serpent?

If ye then, being evil, know to give good gifts unto your children, how much more shall the Father which is in heaven give good things to them that ask him?

Yet ye have not, because ye ask not. – (Matthew 7: 8- 11, James 4: 2, KJV)

Christ often represented the love of the Father in various ways, giving examples in nature as well as in life, often using family life as well. Here we see Him explaining the love of Father God for His children in the answering of prayer, with the love of an earthly father for his children in the answering of a request made by them for something desired, such as bread or fish. These requests are for actual needs. In this Christ was teaching his disciples what was considered by God as an earnest request. I find that the Lord is not concerned with our wants which many times are mainly centered around a point of vanity, but our earnest requests which are centered around an actual need and in so answering, He also provides our desires in concerns with these needs according to His will. For instance: you may need furniture for your place of living. Now in the asking you may also desire that furniture to be something you consider beautiful, feasible, workable, kid friendly, family friendly, nice or functional. Remember, it is the need not the want that is answered, but in answering the need, because He is a loving God and He often does things in a grand or beautifully considerate way, He gives you the best! I have found that these are the prayers that are most answered. As Jesus said in - Matthew 7: 8-11, (KJV), what Father would give his son asking for bread or fish, a stone or a serpent? Being the heavenly Father that He is, He does expect us to ask when we have a need, instead of going out and trying to make something happen for ourselves and possibly getting into trouble because of it. This type of activity just makes life harder for our self and others. Remember, what we do dosn't just effect one it effects all whom we are involved with. Everything God gives comes with peace of mind, body, soul, and spirit, and no strings attached. Isn't that comforting. The Father wants us to ask, and because He loves us and we love Him, as His children, He has given us the right to ask and expect an answer.

✦ Testimonies of the heart:

My daughter's first day of pre-school, I had walked her to school. It was very cold outside and I have never learned to drive and I had no one to take me and my daughter back and forth to pre-school, so, we walked. Most of the time, I would carry her on my back because her little legs would get tired and it was a long way to walk. I had bought her a beautiful thick jean winter coat that was nice and warm on the inside. The coat was blue with red patches here and there that had pretty little white flowers in them tipped the same red and blue colors that were in the coat. I also had found her some matching red, white and blue warm little gloves to go with it so that her hands would stay nice and warm as we walked back and forth from her school. That afternoon I went to pick my daughter up from school. When I went to put her coat on her, I couldn't find her gloves, in requiring of the teacher as to what may have happened to them. I was told that one of the children might have taken them. I was devastated and hurt that this would happen at a time when I had no more money to buy her a pair of new gloves. Knowing that I had to bring her back out in the cold the next day without any gloves for her hands, I started praying and asking the Father in the name of Jesus to please bless me with some more gloves for my daughter. I didn't know how He was going to do it, I just trusted Him for them. I got up the next morning and covered her hands in various warm socks as I had no more gloves to cover them with to keep her hands from getting cold. Across the street from my apartment, was a parking lot. As we crossed the street and began walking by the parking lot, there laying a few feet from the sidewalk in the parking lot facing me was a brand new pair of little girl's winter gloves in the same colors as her coat, red, white, and blue. Looking around, I saw that the parking lot was empty. There were no cars in the lot, nor was there anybody standing around or other children. I quickly picked up the gloves and we started walking again. Thanking God and rejoicing in the provision of the Father, I went on my way. When I returned back home I washed the gloves and dried them and placed them on my daughter's hands the next day. Returning that same day after school to pick up my daughter once again, I found that this pair of gloves had gone missing as well. Frustrated at the fact that this kept happening and my daughter was once again without gloves and still not as of yet being able to afford to purchase another pair of gloves, I was upset to say the least. These were lean times for me and my children. I prayed again and asked the Lord to please bless me once more with a pair of gloves for my daughter. Not sure that He would, I still hoped that He would. The next morning I and daughter once again started out for her school, again I had to place socks on my daughter's hands to keep them warm. As we crossed the street from my apartment, I started looking for the gloves as we walked by the parking lot. There laying in the parking lot in the same spot as I found the last pair of gloves, was another pair of a little girl's gloves in the same colors once again as my daughter's coat, but this time they were leather mittens with a warm fur lining! They were better and warmer and even prettier than the last pair! Grateful and happy about the Lord's providing of the mittens, tearing up, I started jumping up and down in the parking lot and praising God! Once again, the parking lot was completely empty and there was nobody around! This time I prayed and asked the Lord to please not let this pair go missing. I heard the voice of the Lord telling me to pin the gloves far up inside the sleeves of my daughter's coat where they could not be seen or found when I took her coat off. When we got to her school, I remembered what the Spirit of the Lord had told me and I pinned the gloves way up inside her coat sleeves out of sight! This time when I went back to pick up my daughter after school and checked inside the sleeves, there were the mittens! Thankful to God, I gave praise to the Lord Jesus for His provision and wise counsel! Never again did I have to worry about my daughter's gloves coming up missing. I have found that the Lord is even concerned about what we may think are the most minute things, things that may seem small and of little concern to some, but are of great concern to others. God even cares about the hairs on our head;

But even the very hairs of your head are all numbered. Fear not therefore: - (Luke 12:7, KJV)

In James 4:2, KJV, it says;

We have not, because we ask not - James 4:2, KJV.

Do not be afraid to ask the Lord anything in the name of Jesus, an earnest prayer will be given an earnest answer.

And all things, whatsoever ye ask in prayer, believing, ye shall receive. – (Matthew 21: 22, KJV)

The Angel and the Pessimist

"Be not forgetful to entertain strangers: for thereby some have entertained angels unawares.

Are they not all ministering spirits, sent forth to minister for them who shall be heirs of salvation?

And God hearkened to the voice of Manoah; and the angel of God came again unto the woman as she sat in the field: but Manoah her husband was not with her.

And the woman made haste, and ran, and shewed her husband, and said unto him, Behold, the man hath appeared unto me, that came unto me the other day.

And Manoah arose, and went after his wife, and came to the man, and said unto him, Art thou the man that spakest unto the woman? And he said, I am." – Hebrews 13: 2, 1: 14, Judges 13: 8- 11, KJV)

Many times in scripture, though spiritual beings, the angels of God often showed up in the form of man to deliver messages to or do a work for those to whom they had been sent by God the Father too. The pre-incarnate Christ would sometimes appear as well to man in the Old Testament and would be known as the Angel of the LORD. When appearing as a normal man, angels were often not recognized right away until they said or did something that struck the attention or revealed to the individual who they were. Now there are good angels and there are the fallen angels. The angels of the Lord are called ministering spirits and they do the Lord's bidding;

Are they not all ministering spirits, sent forth to minister for them who shall be heirs of salvation? – (Hebrews 1:14, KJV)

The fallen angels who followed Satan, rebelled against God along with Satan, and fell with him out of Heaven;

And the great dragon was cast out, that old serpent, called the Devil, and Satan, which deceiveth the whole world: he was cast out into the earth, and his angels were cast out with him. – (Revelation 12:9, KJV)

Often when the Lord wanted to get the attention of someone in a special way, He would often send an angel in the form of a man. Like the angel He sent to inform Manoah and his wife that they were going have a son. ;

And the angel of the LORD appeared unto the woman, and said unto her, Behold now, thou art barren, and bearest not: but thou shalt conceive, and bear a son.

And the woman made haste, and ran, and shewed her husband, and said unto him, Behold, the man hath appeared unto me, that came unto me the other day, - (Judges 13:3, 10, KJV)

Now today, we live in a world that does not readily accept the eye witness accounts of appearances of angels to an individual or individuals, as easily as they did in the Bible, because so much skepticism has arose in the world due unto non-belief, but this still doesn't stop them from appearing to whomsoever God decides to send them, it is, what it is. Just as in the Bible, the word of God when God sends His angels out today to do His bidding, it is just as amazing today as it was back then when you have an encounter with an angel of the Lord. The affect upon you is still the same, amazing!

✦ Testimonies of the Heart:

In the year 1981, I was going through some things that had me questioning the Lord if He was still with me. Of course God is always with us, but sometimes you could be going through things so pressing and so discouraging, especially if they seem to be going on a length of time. Sometimes the spiritual warfare gets so heavy, you find yourself wondering if God is still with you or is he going to be with you in what you are going through or facing. Now, once again, God is always with us. Now when we find ourselves questioning the fact that God is with us, I find that it is because we have taken our mind off of what the Lord has already revealed, said or shown, and like Peter, we have taken our eyes off of Jesus and have started to look at the wind and the waves instead of keeping our mind's eye focused on Christ. The seed of doubt tries to creep in and throw us off the path in which God is leading us. This is what was happening to me, and if it had been allowed to continue it would have destroyed me. At the time nothing nobody was telling me encouraged me or made sense, I was caught up in the wind and the waves of my circumstances, I had taken my focus off of what the Lord was telling me and looking at my situation instead of my promised victory in Jesus, and the fact, that God was with me and I was not alone.

While walking across the bridge one day that led into downtown, I saw a tall man walking towards me. He was wearing a red plaid rumpled shirt. His hair was shaggy looking and his face looked weathered like he had worked outside all his life. He was wearing some old and worn looking jeans with the cuff folded up. He looked like someone you might expect to have come straight out of the hills or mountains! I immediately was nervous, having had an bad experience with someone who looked like this before while walking to church one night whereas the man tried to pick me up in his truck, and pulled a shotgun out of the window and threaten to shoot me if I did not get in his truck, that night as I stood on the curb holding my Bible open to - Psalm 91, KJV, against my chest, and praying and pleading the blood of Jesus over me to cover and protect me from all hurt harm and danger, God sent two cars with bright lights to shine in the man's windows, revealing him, one sat across from him at the intersection in front of him and one that pulled up in back of him, both cars did not move until the man took off up the hill and away from me, frustrated, the man pulled the gun back inside the truck and told me, I was lucky this time, what he thought he was going to do, God did not let him. The car that was in back of him proceeded to follow him all the way up the hill and beyond until he was out of sight! Thus saving my life! I knew it was angels! No one said a word! The man in the truck pulled his gun back inside the window and took off! The protection, mercy and the grace of God helped me get away that night and run for my life, up the hill to my church and to safety from the 'would be' assailant! I knew those two cars had to be God's angels watching over me because they did not move until the man moved, sitting through several red lights! Not once taking their lights off of him shining at high beam into the man's front and back window of his truck! Making him highly visible to the eyes! When he took off around the corner they took off as well, with the one following behind him up the hill! Neither driver, who I could not see, said a word to me. God saved me that night standing on that curve, praying for my life!

Now here again I was alone. My immediately went back to that night when I was trying to get to church and what happened. I began to think that I might have to make a break for it and run for my life. I looked around over the bridge behind me to see if there was any one having started walking on the bridge that I could run to for help or if there was a car coming that I could flag down in my defense to help me. There was no one and the cars that were coming were driving by me too fast to stop. The man continued to walk toward me with a smile on his face holding a newspaper in his hand. Feeling the fear growing in me, I stopped and looked toward the street to see if I could jump into the street and run across it to the other side without getting hit by a passing car if I had to make a quick getaway if the man tried to grab hold of me. Jumping off the bridge was out of the question without killing myself. I thought about turning around and running back across the bridge and up the hill to where I lived, but the man was too close now, and I thought he might catch up to me. Paralyzed with fear, all kinds of thoughts were going through my mind and the remembrance of what had happened to me that night before came flashing back into my mind. I just stood there and waited for what I thought was sure to be a confrontation. The man kept smiling, I became more and more nervous, if I did not have enough happening in my life, I thought. As the man got closer to me he momentarily stopped and said, I read something funny today in, "Today's Chuckle". Today's Chuckle was a joke put in a corner on the front page of the newspaper about a real truth. It was written to make you laugh about something that by all means should not have been happening, had someone been thinking clearly or doing things right. He shoved the paper in my hands and without another word, walked off without once looking back. I was puzzled to say the least. I turned around and stood watching him until he got to the top of the hill. I watched as he seemed to just walk out of sight. Fear leaving me, when I was assured in my spirit that he had went somewhere far enough away for me to feel safe, I opened up the newspaper and began to read "Today's Chuckle". It said, and I quote, "A pessimist is someone who looks both ways on a one way street!" I found out later that it was a quote by a man called, Dr. Lawrence J. Peter in 1977, it didn't take a PhD to understand who the Lord was revealing the pessimist to be, the pessimist was me. A pessimist is a person who tends to see the worst aspect of things or believe that the worse will happen. I immediately started to pray and ask the Lord "Was that really me?" All in my spirit I heard the Spirit of the Lord say how I had been struggling inside of me whether to believe Him or not, that He was going to do just what He told me and that I was letting my fear of an negative outcome of something that I was going through get the better of me, and that He was with me, and how that I was looking at the situation, going back and forth in my mind about it instead of focusing on what He was revealing to me and telling me. How that my path was set in one direction in him and that was forward, not backward. That He was with me and would always be with me to direct my path, to keep me and to give me the victory. Tears started flowing as a sweet relief, a confidence, and blessed assurance came over my soul and into my spirit. No longer the pessimist, I started walking forward. Yes, that, that I was going through, Jesus brought me through and out and, yes, I did get the victory! I knew then that I had encountered an angel. I often wondered why the Lord would use something that I feared to establish a non- fear in me, but I have come to understand that God's ways are not our ways, maybe it was to establish that sometimes things we fear the most are the things in Him we should not be fearing, especially when we are in His loving and capable hands. Just like that night I was on my way to church. I asked the Lord later, just to assure myself of my experience I asked the Lord if truly I had seen one of His angels to let me see the man again just one more time. Two weeks had gone by. I thought that the Lord was not going to answer my request. I was on the bus one day coming into down town. There were a lot of people walking up and down the sidewalk. Just as the bus was pulling in front of the plaza where the buses lined up to drop off and pick up passengers, I saw him! He was taller than everybody else on the sidewalk. As I stared out the window of the bus at him, he turned and looked at me. Still wearing the same clothes he had on that day I encountered him on the bridge, he smiled at me and waved, I looked, once again paralyzed, but this time with amazement and joy that the Lord had answered my request! Immediately it seemed as if he became swallowed up by the crowd, how? I don't know because he was taller than everybody else!! I jumped off the bus as soon as it stopped and made my way back through the crowd trying to find him and but he was gone. I knew without a doubt I had met an angel of God that day. Since then I have become a firm believer that, yes, God is still sending His angels into this world to do His bidding and yes, the Lord is still confirming His faithful care and concern over us and for us every day of our lives.

I waited patiently for the LORD; and He inclined unto me, and heard my cry. – (Psalm 40: 1, KJV)

Just a little Mud

"And when He had thus spoken, He spat on the ground, and He anointed the eyes of the blind man with the clay,

And said unto him, Go, wash in the pool of Siloam, (which is by interpretation, Sent.) He went his way therefore, and washed, and came seeing." – (John 9: 6 - 7, KJV)

Christ when healing the people, often used different methods. Some He just spoke a word and they were healed, some He touched, some He used His own divine saliva to heal. This particular blind man, Christ made clay out of His own saliva and the dirt from the ground. After applying it to the man's eyes, told him to go and wash in the pool of Siloam. Now we know that Christ could have just spoke the word and the man would have been healed, but He choose to spit into the dirt and make clay instead, and then to send the man to the pool of Siloam to wash the clay from his eyes in order to receive his sight. One has to wonder why the extended means in order for the man to receive his sight. When you read the rest of the story in John chapter 9, (KJV), you find that later this same man was brought before the Pharisees in question of how he received his sight. This one act of healing allowed the once blind man to become a witness unto Christ before the unbelieving Pharisees and not only that, but when Jesus met up with the man later, this same man became a follower of Christ. Now you would think that would have been the end of the story but it goes on. Once again there were Pharisees standing around Christ that heard when He asked the man whose sight was healed John 9:38, (KJV):

Jesus heard that they had cast him out; and when He had found him, He said unto him, Dost thou believe on the Son of God? – John 9:35, (KJV)

On finding out that it was Christ who stood before him gave this answer in John 9:38, (KJV);

And He said, Lord, I believe. And he worshipped Him - (John 9: 38, KJV).

The act of faith expressed by the man in Christ and the healing and the method of healing that was done by Christ, all came into play towards the winning of many souls that were to be gained by Christ later. Christ choose to test the man's faith, by testing him to see if he would be obedient to Him and do as He asked and go and wash in the pool in order to receive his healing. In so doing strengthened the man's faith and belief in Christ. This one act of the testing of his faith and trust in Christ led to the man's soul salvation and no doubt may have led to the saving salvation of many others afterwards that either knew or had heard of the miraculous way the man had received his sight from Christ. I have found that every mercy, every grace, every blessing, favor, miracle and healing that the Lord does for us, serves a far greater purpose than we could ever imagine or realize. I am sure when the man was healed and later believed on Christ never thought that his miracle and new found belief in Christ as the Son of God, would be the catalyst for many others coming to believe in Christ also. When he asked the Pharisees that were questioning him, would they be Christ's disciples also? I am sure it had to have caused quite a stir amongst the unbelieving Pharisees, because here was an undeniable miracle of God! This one man's testimony and healing was recorded and written down for all eternity as a witness unto the fact that Jesus Christ truly, was and is the Anointed One, the Son of God! What a declaration! All from just a little mud!

✦ Testimonies of the Heart:

In the year 1991 I had went to get my eyes examined as I would usually do when I felt I needed a stronger prescription. I had been seeing a great deal of black spots in my eyes and my eyesight seemed to be growing increasingly blurry, it was like trying to look through black polka dots, with blurred vision with and without glasses. My thinking was that I just needed a new pair. After having my eyes examined, I received some very solemn news. I was told that I was going blind and would soon need a seeing eye dog to get around and I would have to go to school to learn Braille and that there was nothing that could be done about it due unto the extent of the damage to my eyes! I was given the name of a school for the blind that I was to register to, so that I could learn Braille and how to live or operate in my life being blind. I was told that an appointment would be made for me to go and get set up in the school. I left the office and just sunk down inside. I couldn't believe that the God I served who had done so many miracles in my life, would let me go blind, time to pray.

I went to the church that afternoon to clean as I usually did during the week. While there I went to the altar and cried out to the Lord in the mighty name of Jesus, and asked Him to please heal my eyes so that I would not become blind for the rest of my life. I heard the Spirit of the Lord tell me to place my glasses on the altar for two years, and at the end of two years, He would heal my eyes. That following Sunday, I went up to my pastor and told him what the Lord had given me to do after I prayed about the doctor's report and my having to apply for a school for the blind and if it was alright to place my glasses on the altar? He told me that if I had that kind of faith, then it was ok with him. He willing agreed to put my glasses on the top shelf of the wooden podium on which he preached from. Often when our pastor was praying over written requests on the altar, this is where he placed them. Many in the church ridiculed me for placing my glasses on the altar for two years like the Lord told me. Often questioning me if I was sure I heard from the Lord, being as to how I was going completely blind at the time. I stood by what I heard the day I cried out to God for healing for my eyes, I trusted Him. I did not go and sign up for the school of the blind, nor did I sign up to receive a Seeing Eye dog, nor did I return back unto the eye doctor until the two years ended. As the days and months went by, I had to learn how to get around my house and to get to church, as it seemed as if my eyesight got worse before it became better. The church was in walking distance and my son helped me count the steps it took me to get there. I had to learn to see without seeing with my hands, ears, smell and feet. I would stand at the curb, listening for the sounds of the different vehicles that went up and down the street. At home I used touch to feel my way around, counting my steps as I went. All during the period of the two years, I was constantly questioned and ridiculed for my act of faith in God. Even told that I could not have heard what I heard because I still could not see. Then one day right before the period of the two years were to end, I started noticing the blurriness going away, I was seeing the light of day better and the spots becoming less and less as each day went by. Then one day at the end of the two years, I woke up and my eyes were cleared of all spots and the dark blurriness, in fact my eyesight had improved! Hallelujah! Much to the surprise of everyone including all the skeptics that had consistently ridiculed me and told me, I must have heard wrong. I then scheduled an appointment to go back to the eye doctor. When I stepped back into the office I was asked what happened to me? That an appointment had been set up for me to get into the school for the blind and I never got back in touch with them or went to the appointment. I asked if I could be examined again, they did. After examining me, I was asked, what doctor had I been too, and what procedure had been performed for my eyes? They further went on to say that there was no more damage in my eyes and that I was seeing better than before I first came to the office! I shared with them what the Lord had told me to do and that was how I was now able to see without the spots and the darkness in my eyes. The report was not accepted with the joy I thought it would be accepted in fact I was told not to come back again! Yes, I can totally relate to the man whose sight was healed by Christ. Why two years? When Christ could have healed my eyes immediately? I can only say that it was a testing of my faith and a faith builder, a lesson in patience, a providing of a witness of the healing power and the promises of God. Through it I was able to share a testimony of faith in God, and the reward of patience and waiting on God. I never stopped serving my Lord just because a part of me was disabled I used it to get stronger in Christ Jesus. I continued to serve because one thing I knew, my God loved me, and I loved Him! The wondrous miracle He did for me, I shared it across the country as well as in my own church and I have seen it be a blessing to many to inspire others to believe for their miracle in Christ Jesus our Lord and Savior. Today as I share what the Lord did for me so many years ago. My faith builder at that time was a pair of glasses put on the altar, and left there for 2 years. The man in the Bible was just a little mud put on the eyes by the Son of God! And a washing in the pool of Siloam!

Jesus answered and said unto them, Go and shew John again those things which ye do hear and see;

The blind receive their sight, and the lame walk, the lepers are cleansed, and the deaf hear, the dead are raised up, and the poor have the gospel preached to them.

And blessed is he, whosoever shall not be offended in me. – (Matthew 11: 4 -6, KJV)

WALKING ON WATER

And straightway Jesus constrained His disciples to get into a ship, and to go before Him unto the other side, while He sent the multitudes away.

But the ship was now in the midst of the sea, tossed with waves: for the wind was contrary.

And in the fourth watch of the night Jesus went unto them, walking on the sea.

And when the disciples saw Him walking on the sea, they were troubled, saying, It is a spirit; and they cried out for fear.

But straightway Jesus spake unto them, saying, Be of good cheer; it is I be not afraid.

And Peter answered Him and said, Lord, if it be thou, bid me come unto Thee on the water.

And He said, Come. And when Peter was come down out of the ship, he walked on the water, to go to Jesus. – (Matthew 14: 22, 24-29, KJV)

In this passage of scriptures, you read where Jesus compelled the disciples to go before Him in the ship to the other side of the sea. Now at no time did He tell them He would follow later in another ship. He just told them to go while He went up the mountain by Himself to pray. Then, while in prayer talking to the Father, He saw in the spirit His disciples at their wits and strength's end trying to get across the sea. The wind was blowing against them coming from the other side of the lake or sea, so they had to row against the wind in order to try and make it across. Now Peter and most of the other disciples were no strangers to the sea, being experienced fishermen, no doubt having had to face weather conditions out on the sea that were not always amiable to them. This particular occasion, nothing they knew about the sea or their situation was helping them. Sometimes we run into those circumstances or situations where nothing we know or can do apart from God can help us. They were out on the water in the midst of the storm in the need of help. Jesus seeing their struggle while on the mountain praying, with the wind and waves came down the mountain and walked across the waters toward them. Peter when he saw that it was Jesus who asked Him to bid him to come to him. Jesus told him to come. It was a test of faith for Peter and an opportunity to reveal the divinity of Christ in that He was both God and man as brought out in Philippians 2: 6 – 7, KJV;

Who, being in the form of God, thought it not robbery to be equal with God:

But made himself of no reputation, and took upon Him the form of a servant, and was made in the likeness of men: - Philippians 2: 6 - 7, (KJV)

The fact that Jesus allowed him to walk on the water no doubt paved the way for Peter believing in Jesus Christ for the impossible and proved to Peter that Jesus could do anything, it wasn't until Peter took his eyes off of Jesus while walking on the waters, he begin to sink;

But when he saw the wind boisterous, he was afraid; and beginning to sink, he cried, saying, LORD, save. - (Matthew 14: 30, KJV)

This miracle and wonder of Christ bidding him to come and enabling Peter to walk on the water in the midst of the waves and the wind raging around them, stands as a testimony to all of what can be accomplished through faith and a word from our Lord and Savior, Jesus Christ and of the help we can believe God for, and the situation calling for it. Sometimes in our lives the Lord just wants to establish in us that He is the God of the impossible! By making it possible, through Him! The adversary would love to have us believe that the Lord is not doing wonders and miracles like He did in the Bible anymore, but I am here as a witness and a recipient of miracles, God is doing miracles!

For with God nothing shall be impossible. – (Luke 1: 37, KJV)

✦ Testimonies of the Heart:

One year, I was violently attacked where I was beaten and punched continuously until I was unconscious. It caused me to have two concussions and the discs in my neck and spine had become pressed in and pinched in the back of the neck and mid spine from the offense. When I came too, I heard the Spirit of the Lord telling me to call for help because I had a head and neck injury. I called for help, having had to go to emergency and then later to a specialist, a neurologist, because my whole body had started to slow down and it became increasingly difficult to move.

When I made an appointment to see a doctor, I was then sent to a specialist. After having MRI's taken and other exams and scans, I was told as I was losing the ability to use my legs and my arms and that I was slowly becoming paralyzed, and in a matter of months, I would be completely paralyzed. I went into prayer, I asked the Lord to please let me not to become paralyzed. While I was praying, I heard the Spirit of the Lord tell me, that if I did what He said and moved to where He was telling me to go, He would give me a, walking on water miracle! I asked the Lord, what did He mean by a, Walking on water miracle, He told me that He let His Son, Jesus, walk on the waters, as if He was walking on dry land. He said the wind was still blowing, the waves were still raging, but it did not stop Jesus from walking across the waters as if He were walking on dry land. He further went on to say, He would not heal me, but He would bless me to live, to walk and to work as if there was nothing wrong with me. I told the Lord, Yes, and that at His word I would do what He said. I did and God did just what He said. After I moved, I went to the doctor in the city I was living in and told them what had happened to me, because I wanted to see for myself and confirm the miracle in myself what God promised me if I moved. I was scheduled for more exams and scans there as well. When the results came in, I was scheduled to come in to see a neurologist. When I was called back into the office, I was asked how I was feeling, I told them, they then became very quiet and just sat and stared at me for a few minutes. I admit it made me nervous because I didn't know why they were just sitting and staring at me, was there bad news or what? Finally, after feeling somewhat uncomfortable and curious as to why they were just sitting and staring at me, I asked if everything was alright. They answered and said that they were just trying to figure out how I walked into their office by myself and how I was not in a wheelchair? They took the pictures out of their folder of my spine and set them up in the lights, pointing out the discs that were pressed into my spinal cord in my neck almost flattening it to the point whereas the cord appeared to be real thin, which by all rights should have caused me to be paralyzed from my neck down, but God! I saw that the MRI'S and the x-rays were the same as the pictures that were taken at the hospital in the previous state. I was amazed myself and excited at the witness of the walking on water miracle God had given me through obedience to His will and His word to me, I felt encouraged and emboldened to share my testimony with the doctor of the goodness of God and the walking on water miracle, how God took that same principle of faith that was in His Son, our Savior and applied it to my spine, was just an absolute miracle! Amazed, they then went on further to say, that according to the results of the MRI, I was should be paralyzed from my neck on down, and not be able to move from the neck down! They acknowledged that it truly was a miracle of God and I can say all due unto Jesus and the promise of a walking on water miracle!

And when He saw them, He said unto them, Go shew yourselves unto the priests. And it came to pass, that, as they went, they were cleansed. – (Luke 17: 14, KJV)

SPECIAL MIRACLES

"And God wrought special miracles by the hands of Paul:

So that from his body were brought unto the sick handkerchiefs or aprons, and the diseases departed from them, and the evil spirits went out of them." – (Acts 19:11, 12, KJV)

And he said, bring me a new cruse, and put salt therein. And they brought it to him.

And he went forth unto the spring of waters, and cast the salt in there, and said, Thus saith the LORD, I have healed these waters; there shall not be from thence any more death or barren land. – (2 Kings 2: 20, 21, KJV)

And one went into the field to gather herbs, and found a wild vine, and gathered thereof wild gourds his lap full, and came and shred them into the pot of pottage: for they knew them not.

So they poured out for the men to eat. And it came to pass, as they were eating of the pottage, that they cried out, and said, O thou man of God, there is death in the pot. And they could not eat thereof.

But he said, Then bring meal. And he cast it into the pot; and he said, Pour out for the people, that they may eat. And there was no harm in the pot. – (2 Kings 4: 39-41, KJV)

In the book of Acts, we see special or unusual miracles being performed through the Apostle Paul by God for the sick and for the casting out of evil spirits. Now these were unusual indeed considering the time period in which they were performed. Jesus had already risen, as told in Mark 16:19, (KJV);

So then after the Lord had spoken unto them, He was received up into heaven, and sat on the right hand of God. – (Mark 16:19, KJV)

Unlike in the Old Testament when unusual and special miracles performed by the prophets of old, such as the waters purified by salt and poisonous food had been been made not poisonous by meal, were more expected than they were at this particular time. As each generation passes, ones' expectations pass as well, which is one reason why there is such a need for the renewing of the mind and spirit.

Paul could not get to everyone to lay hands on them in prayer for them to be healed or delivered from sickness, disease or evil spirits, so he placed handkerchiefs and aprons upon his body and prayed over them that the Lord's blessing would be with them and over them, no doubt anointing them with oil as well, this special miracle was recorded in - Acts 19:11 – 12, (KJV);

And God wrought special miracles by the hands of Paul:

So that from his body were brought unto the sick handkerchiefs or aprons, and the diseases departed from them, and the evil spirits went out of them. – (Acts 19:11 – 12, KJV)

These types of miracles were considered special and unusual since they did not come from the individual that was praying, physically laying hands on the person that was sick or afflicted. Instead it was done through a point of contact, such as the handkerchiefs. These points of contacts were prayed over and then anointed with oil, some like this particular point of contact the handkerchiefs were laid on Paul's body. Paul was so anointed by the Holy Spirit that, that the anointing that was on him was transferred to the cloths that were laid on his body and when the people accepted them in faith and believing for the Lord to work through the point of contact, they were healed. So what we see is faith touching faith in the name of Jesus through a point of contact bringing about special miracles. Jesus said in John 14:13 – 14, (KJV), attesting to the fact that when we pray in His name, our prayers are heard;

And whatsoever ye ask in my name, that I will do, that the Father may be glorified in the Son.

If ye shall ask any thing in my name, I will do it. – John 14: 13 – 14, (KJV)

✦ Testimonies of the Heart:

Some years ago, between the years of 1987 and 1990, I cannot remember the exact year our Pastor, who also was an Evangelist had been asked to come and speak at a church down state from us. Often when our pastor would be asked to speak anywhere in the state, the church would usually follow him. This time though we did not have many drivers. So the pastor rented a van from another minister friend of his. The van was not in good shape, it was very rusty in places and in some spots along the floor on the inside, it had even rusted completely through, you could see the road, and the motor spurted at times. We all piled up in the van anyway, hoping to get to church and back home safely and on time. We covered the holes with mats and were careful not to put our feet on them. Talk about risking life and limb to go to church, we did. Our pastor was a very anointed and powerful speaker, and the church loved hearing him speak and watching the Holy Spirit work through him towards blessing the people. It was a joy following him to the meetings, because we knew we were going to get the opportunity to see God work! About and hours down the road, because it was going to take us couple of hours to get there, fumes started coming up into the van through the holes in the floor of the van from the exhaust system. I was sitting in the back of the van where the holes in the floor of the van were. My head started

55

throbbing just like it would if I was having a bad sinus headache. I was becoming very nauseated and sick to my stomach. The fumes were very strong. I told the one of the members how sick I was becoming, they told me to roll the window down a little bit, so I did. After having it down a bit, I was told to roll it back up because it was cold and others were complaining about the air coming from the window, it was winter. So I had to roll it back up. I started getting sicker and sicker, I felt myself like I was losing consciousness. I took my anointing oil out of my purse and held it to my chest and prayed for the Lord to take the fumes coming from the van's exhaust out of my lungs. It felt like my breath was getting shorter and shorter and I was becoming sleepier and sleepier, as if being drugged to sleep. I was afraid that if the Lord didn't help me, and I fell asleep, I might not wake up. I prayed all the more harder while holding the bottle of oil to my chest. I did not open it because I did not want it to spill in the van, because the ride was very bumpy, so I kept it closed tight. Others complained of smelling the fumes mildly, but that they were not getting sick, I was the only one. I was told to hold on until we got to church. I continued to pray and ask the Lord to take the fumes out of my lungs. I fought to stay conscious and to keep from falling asleep. I noticed later that my breathing had gotten better and I was able to take deep breathes and the smell of the fumes had gotten lighter, I thought that I had become so full of the fumes that I was getting ready to die, as to the reason why they had become lighter. All of a sudden the van spurted and the engine cut off. We ended up coasting to the side of the road. The Pastor called for a tow truck to come and we all got out of the van. I was still holding my bottle of anointing oil in my hand. As I went to put my oil back in my purse because we were all standing outside of the van on the side of the road and it was so cold and I didn't want my oil to freeze, I noticed a plume of gray smoke swirled around the inside of the bottle and congregating on the bottom inside the bottle. Curious to see what it was, because when I placed my oil in my purse before the trip, it was clear. I opened the bottle to get a better look at what it was. Immediately to my surprise and awe, a smell of the carbon monoxide that I had been breathing in the van came out of the oil like a cloud. I could not see how this was possible since the top was screwed down tight whereas nothing could get in or out of the bottle. But there it was like a plume of gray smoke swirled around the inside of the bottle to the bottom of the bottle as if someone had poured it in there for all to see. I quickly went and showed it to my pastor who questioned me if I had opened the bottle at any time. I told him how that I never opened the bottle because I didn't want it to spill out and how that I made sure the top was screwed on tight before I put it in my purse because I didn't want it to leak out. He was amazed and asked me if he could show it to the others and the ministers that had he had called to come and pick us up from the side of the road. I told him how that I was becoming sicker and sicker in the van from smelling the fumes coming from the exhaust through the hole in the floor in front of where I was sitting in the van, and how that I prayed and asked the Lord to take the fumes out of my lungs. I also shared how that later as we traveled down the road before the van stopped, I seemed to get better. I told him how I thought that I had just become so full that I was going to fall asleep and not wake up and how that I fought it and kept on praying. I didn't know that God was drawing the fumes out of my lungs just like I had asked him into the oil, while and with the top screwed on tight! Everyone that saw and smelled the fumes in the oil and heard my testimony marveled at the unusual miracle of the oil and the fumes, but there it was in plain sight for all to see!! And smell!! God drew the fumes into the oil so that they would not make me go unconscious, saving my life that day. My pastor asked me if he could set my oil on the altar for all to see who came into the sanctuary to see for their selves a testimony and visual witness of the miracles and the wonders of God. I said yes, grateful unto God and grateful to still be alive because of Him drawing the fumes of the carbon monoxide out of my lungs that day and into the oil that I had kept pressed to my chest while we were on the road. Is God still doing amazing special and unusual miracles today just like He did back then? Yes, He is!

ONE BASKET OF FRUIT

And it shall come to pass, that before they call, I will answer; and while they are yet speaking, I will hear. – (Isaiah 65:24, KJV)

There are times when we pray that the Lord answers our prayers, while we are yet praying them. Now it is up to the Lord when He wants or decides to answer our prayers. Now of course we would love for the Lord to answer our prayer requests quickly, but not all of the time is it necessary for Him to do so. A Lot of times we may feel this way, because of some emotional distress, or weariness of spirit when we are going through some trial or testing by the adversary to see if we will hold to our faith in Christ and our Father God. Not always is it an immediate need for the Lord to step in and give us answer according to what we are asking. Everything is not always an immediate need, but there are times when there is an immediate need. It is these times when the Lord shows up suddenly, that still amazes us, because it establishes the fact that, yes, we are praying to a very real God that truly sees our struggles and if seeing the need, will answer quickly. Many I know don't want to believe we serve a true and living Savior, and a awesome and powerful God that answers prayers just like it is recorded in the word of God, but the fact of the matter is, we do, and just like in Bible times, we serve a Savior today that has not changed, and what I love about Him, is that He is still answering our most urgent of prayers. Why? Because He loves us and His word will not go out and come back void;

So shall my word be that goeth forth out of my mouth: it shall not return unto me void, but it shall accomplish that which I please, and it shall prosper in the thing whereto I sent it. – (Isaiah 55: 11, KJV)

✦ Testimonies of the Heart:

One day as I sat in my living room praying, asking the Lord to bless me and my children with some fruit to help stretch the food that I had on hand. My children loved fruit and I didn't believe in feeding them a lot of candy to snack on in between meals, plus I wanted something that was going to really fill them as well as be healthy for them too. I usually keep a lot of fruit on hand but this time I didn't and I didn't have any more money to go and buy more. I put my faith in God and in my Lord and Savior Jesus Christ to answer my prayer, hoping and believing that He was listening and would have mercy and would do just that. Now I didn't know how He was going to answer the prayer, all I knew was that I needed it answered and quickly. I just needed an answer as quick as He could give it to me, because I was running out of food with no means of replacing it. I put out a cry of desperation to the Lord in hopes that I would receive an answer as soon as possible. Now let me say this, it is the Lord's goodwill to answer us when He sees fit, but the fact that He answers us at all, shows His great love, mercy, kindness, and compassion for His people because the truth is; none of us in our best state are really living a life that is really worthy of a most pure and Holy God and Savior, but for His love for us, we are blessed. As I sat on the sofa in my living room crying my heart out to the Lord to please bless me with some fruit for my children, a knock came at my door while I was praying. Feeling somewhat annoyed that someone would be knocking at my door while I was in the midst of tears thinking about my present situation and desperately crying out to the Lord for help. I started not to answer the knock at my door, but I heard a voice in my spirit telling me to get up quickly and answer the door. With tears still wet on my cheeks, I jumped up off the sofa and ran over to the door, unlocking it and pulling it open quickly I saw a man running down the steps. I stayed on the second floor in an apartment building and the steps were right in front of the door of my apartment. There in front of my door was this huge fruit gift basket with all kinds of fruit and all of them were the favorite fruits I and my children loved to eat! I was totally surprised and caught off guard. This was the first time I had experienced or recognized how swiftly the Lord answered prayer before I could finish praying about what I was asking for Him to do. Amazing! I found out later that the man I saw running down the stairs when I opened my door was a resident that stayed in the same apartment building as me and my children were staying. The Lord had placed it upon a total stranger's heart, who did not even know me nor I him, to buy a basket of fruit and place it at my door! Talk about the goodness of God! Seeing the neighbor trying to run down the stairs, I called out to him to wait! Realizing that I had caught him before he could get down the stairs, he stopped and dropped his head and confessed how that he was trying to get out of sight before I could open the door and catch him leaving the basket at my door. He told me how that he only knocked because he wanted me to know the basket was there so that no one would come along and take the basket seeing that it was left at my door and had not been picked up. I thanked him, recognizing that the Spirit of the Lord must have moved upon him to do what he did, I began questioning him. There was no mistaking that this was a direct answer to my prayer unto the Lord for the fruit! I asked him, how he knew I needed the fruit? (Especially since I was just praying and asking the Lord for it as he was knocking on the door.) He answered and said that he did not know I needed the fruit. He went on further to say how that he was walking downtown and just as he was about to pass this store that made the baskets, he heard a voice in his mind, telling him to stop and go inside and buy the fruit basket and give it to the woman upstairs for her and her children. He said that he started to keep going, thinking that it was just his mind playing tricks on him, but then he heard the voice again. This time though, the voice spoke even firmer and louder, go inside and buy a fruit basket for the woman upstairs, for her and her children! He said that it was so strong in fact that he felt compelled to obey it! Talk about God answering prayer! He went on further to say that he bought the basket with the intentions of setting it at my door and leaving since he knew I did not know him and would might think it strange that a total stranger was sitting a basket of fruit at my door. He would have been right, had I not knew my Lord and how good He is to His people. He said he had never experienced anything like that before and it really shook him and got his attention to hear a voice like that speaking to him so strongly in his mind, especially since he was not thinking anything like that when it happened. He said he had just got off of work and was walking downtown on his way to a restaurant to buy him a sandwich and some sides to take home with him and eat for his dinner when he heard the voice as he was passing the shop telling him to stop, and go inside and buy the fruit. Looking at the embarrassed expression on his face and realizing that he truly did not know why the urgency that was put upon him to do what he did, gave me an opportunity to witness to the young man about the Lord Jesus Christ and how the Lord intervenes at times on our behalf especially when we pray and ask him too. The young man said he now understood who it was that spoke to him and why it was so strong. This conversation led to many about our Lord and Savior Jesus Christ, ending in the young man getting saved, giving his life to the Lord Jesus Christ and joining our church. The young man became a faithful witness of our Lord and Savior, so much until our pastor made him his right hand man or armor bearer as we say in the church and followed him on many speaking engagements when our pastor had been asked to come and minister. This all came about through the goodness of the Lord and the answering of a prayer before the prayer was finished! It led to the saving of a soul, the establishing one's faith in Jesus Christ and the power and the witness of God being magnified because of one selfless act of kindness by a stranger, a family in a desperate need, provided for, proving that beyond a shadow of doubt, God listens to prayer, all prayer that is made from the heart. Thankful and very much grateful for what the Lord did through a neighbor while praying for a little fruit to stretch a meal to feed my children, as I was young in the faith, and still learning the ways of God, to me, what I took away most from this experience, is how the Lord answered the greater need of the soul. Jesus used the answer to prayer concerning the need for the natural fruit to feed my children to give a greater answer concerning the spiritual need of the soul of one of His children; the fruit of salvation; the results, a changed life! All this came from answered prayer and a gift of, one basket of fruit!

Ask and it shall be given you; seek, and you shall find; knock, and it shall be opened unto you: – (Matthew 7: 7, KJV)

A Moment of Praise

Praise ye the LORD, Praise God in His sanctuary; praise Him in the firmament of His power.

Praise Him for His mighty acts: praise Him according to His excellent greatness.

Praise Him with the sound of trumpet: praise Him the Psaltery and harp.

Praise Him with the timbrel and dance: praise Him with stringed instruments and organs.

Praise Him upon the loud cymbals: Praise Him upon the high sounding cymbals.

Let everything that hath breath praise the LORD. Praise ye the LORD. – (Psalm 150: 1 – 6, KJV)

We are called upon to give praise unto the LORD for all that He is and all that there is therein. All are commanded to Praise God! The Lord loves praise, He loves sound of our voices when we sing and give praise unto His name and He loves the sound of the instruments when they are played in accordance to His praise! It is said in Psalm 22:3, (KJV), that God inhabits the praises of the people;

But Thou art holy, O Thou that inhabitest the praises of Israel. – (Psalm 22:3, KJV)

In - Psalm 100: 1, 4, (KJV), we are called to make a joyful noise unto the Lord and enter His gates with praise;

Make a joyful noise unto the LORD, all ye lands.

Enter into His gates with thanksgiving, and His courts with praise: be thankful unto Him and bless His name. – (Psalm 100: 1, 4, KJV)

✦ TESTIMONIES OF THE HEART:

One day after I had got off of work, I was in no hurry to get back home. There was still a lot of daylight and I just wanted to take a walk through downtown while waiting on my bus to come. It was a beautiful day. It was early fall, the air was that just right temperature, not too cold nor too hot, just right. As I was walking along, I began to hear the church bells play from the church that sat just up the hill from downtown Akron. As I was walking along main street praying, and just thanking God and giving Him the praise in my heart for such a beautiful day. My heart was full and my soul was glad and listening to the church song that was being played by the bells, just made me all the more, happier. The song "Blessed Assurance", (a song written by a blind hymn writer named Fanny Crosby to the music of Phoebe Knapp in 1873), was being played by the bells that days. One of my favorite hymns sung in the church. I began to notice that it seemed as if the bells were all that I could hear. Stopping in the middle of one the wide sidewalks that were down town, I noticed I couldn't hear the cars any more, nor the buses or trucks, or people walking or talking, birds, nothing, but the song that was being played by the bells. It was if God had stopped all the other sounds around me just so I could hear the song being played in His praise and honor. It was amazing! I first thought that something was wrong with my hearing. I kept looking around turning here and there to see if I could hear anybody or anything else, once again, nothing, but the bells of the church. I looked into the people's mouths that were walking around me. I could see their lips moving and their reaction to one another as they carried on a conversation, but there was no sound coming out of their mouth! I walked over unto the curb trying to hear the noise of the cars going by me, but once again there was no sound, nothing! Nothing but that glorious praise unto God from the ringing of the bells! It was beautiful! Having never experienced something like that before, I felt honored that the Lord shared that moment with me just to hear the bells all by themselves without no interference from the surrounding sounds, God blocked out everything, just for me and it was one of my favorite hymns being played! That's why I praise Him! The little things that everyone else may look over, God cares so much for each and every one of us to remember even the songs He knows makes us happy! The Spirit of the Lord gave me the honor of enjoying it all by myself in the midst of a bustling noisy downtown. God's peace fell over the air as the sound of the bells beautiful music reverberated all through the air. It was like a private concert being played just for my benefit. Who could not praise a God that takes so much care just to let you know, He is with you and He hears and receives your praises of Him! It was like the Holy Spirit was answering the praises of my heart unto the Lord, by allowing me hear the bells beautiful melody being played in perfect peace. All without the interference of having to hear the honking of car horns, and the voices of the people talking around me, not even the cooing of the pigeons that frequently walked the sidewalks alongside the people looking for crumbs of food that may have fallen to the ground from people eating and walking along the sidewalk at the same time could be heard. It was as I said before, simply amazing! A sweet and devoted moment of praise to our God and our Lord and Savior Jesus Christ, and a way made to enjoy that praise! What can I say? If God can stop the sun from going down giving Joshua and Israel time so that they could defeat their enemies, and possess the Promised land certainly He can block out the noise of the city that surrounded me so that I could hear the bells alone playing in perfect praise unto Him when He wanted me to hear something very beautiful and anointed from Him. The song of the bells truly blessed me that day, inspiring me to hope for brighter things in Jesus and reminded me of how loving and how great our God is and the blessed assurance that Christ brings to our souls when we give our lives to Him. Jesus is that blessed assurance that was sent from Heaven unto the world to redeem us from sin and turn our hearts back again to the Father who truly loves us and wants us back in His good graces again, there are times that God can and God will, give us, just a moment of perfect praise in Him!

Let every thing that hath breath praise the LORD. Praise ye the LORD." – (Psalm 150: 6, KJV)

APPLES OF GOLD IN PICTURES OF SILVER

A word fitly spoken is like apples of gold in pictures of silver.

– (Proverbs 25: 11, KJV)

Apples of gold in pictures of silver, this brings to mind what these particular colors and symbols and expressions meant. Gold as we have come to understand represents God's glory, whereas silver represents His redemption. The apple in the hands of Jesus is said to represent love, life, knowledge, beauty, and spiritual growth. It is to my understanding that seeing as to how Solomon penned it as words that are fitly spoken, meaning, the right words spoken at the right time were like apples of gold in pictures of silver, and was a thing of beauty, spoken at just the right moment, in just the right situation by the leading of the Lord. God knows what we need to hear when we need to hear it, and yes, when spoken and received in its meaning and purpose, it is the utmost of beauty and to be received with joy and praises unto God for the results it brings in the individual's life, mind, soul and spirit who is receiving it. The glory of God that is invoked in one's spirit by words that are fitly spoken on time by the guidance or the leading of the Holy Spirit, once accepted, brings about a releasing in one's mind and spirit from bondages that have been placed on us by the enemy and a freedom that can only be experienced once these bonds have been broken by a right now word from the Holy Spirit. Words do have power, this is the gold. The apple is a very refreshing fruit that when received, this is the outcome, the glory of God and the purpose of God, revealed in one's life when these timely words are spoken. The silver represents the redeeming qualities that are added unto what is being given through the words spoken, which is the breaking free. The redemption of the person's soul, mind and spirit upon receiving the words of God, not only brings joy to the receiver, but joy to the messenger that the Lord is using to deliver the word as well. When we speak what the Holy spirit places in our heart, and on our tongue to speak unto whomever He leads us to speak to, and it is received and taken to heart, it refreshes the soul, like a sweet juicy apple on a hot day, for both the receiver and the messenger, bringing about a refreshing not only to the body, but also to the soul, thus the pictures of silver, Apples of gold in pictures of silver.

✦ TESTIMONIES OF THE HEART:

Some years back, I was asked to accompany and to minister with another minister in a prayer and Bible study meeting which was hosted by a prison ministry in which she was a part of. I was told that I was free to minister in whatever way the Holy Spirit led me. I had never ministered before in a prison ministry, so I was a little nervous at first, but because I was asked to accompany them and to minister with them as well, I agreed to go. I remember as I got to the door of the room in which we were given to hold the Prayer and Bible study meeting in, I stepped inside the doorway and immediately, I had a vision given me by the Holy Spirit. I saw a big gold throne, about half the height of the wall coming down through the ceiling draped in purple and gold curtains. The curtains stretched out covering the whole front wall of the room. The chair shined a beautiful bright golden light. I heard the voice of the Lord speaking to me over the throne saying, "My presence is now in this room, call it no more a prison, but my House, and treat it as so!" That was all the Holy Spirit had to say to me, my nervousness left me as I submitted to the Lord's will, being replaced by an Holy Ghost boldness! From that point on it this was the Lord's House! I could feel the fire of the Spirit of the Lord burning and rising up inside of me, and the power of God moving inside of me to go forth!! It was all I could do to contain myself while I waited on the other minister to end her class and turn the meeting over to me! Talk about Holy Ghost fire breaking out in the room! We started out with just few women, which soon ended up being a packed room as the Spirit of the Lord began to move, and more outside in the hallway waiting to get in! It was phenomenal! Holy Ghost showed up and showed out! It may have been a prison by material standards, but not that day! It was God's House! And He set off a fire in the Spirit in that place that burned all through the halls!! We were only supposed to be there an hour, but the Spirit of God set things in such an uproar in the Spirit that night, we were allowed to stay two hours and more over our time that we were supposed to there!! Young and old were coming to be prayed for and to hear a word from the Lord, so much until the two of us alone were not able by ourselves to handle the number of women coming for prayer. I heard the Spirit of the Lord speaking to me too ask if there was anyone saved in the crowd, an older woman spoke up whom I came to understand had received Jesus as her Lord and Savior while there. I asked her if she would be willing to be an altar worker for the Lord that night, she agreed, and we went to work for the Lord! I anointed her with anointing oil. I always carried a small bottle with me in my purse wherever I went for times I might need it and prayed for God's anointing to cover her and to equip her with

His Holy Ghost power to help us in prayer with the others. There were many that night were being slain in the Spirit, coming up delivered, some were being filled with the joy of the Lord, praising and shouting and giving honor to God. Some were breaking down in tears and seeking the Lord's forgiveness of their sins, some came for prayer for deliverance from addictions, and so forth! It was truly God's house that night and He was in charge! The Spirit of the Lord was moving so powerfully in that room that night in until the whole room looked like it was lit up with fire and the Glory of God! As the Holy Spirit gave a word for the different individuals who came up for prayer, I could see in the spirit, bondages being broken off their spirit and minds, like chains falling to the ground! Burdens being lifted like heavy yokes off the shoulders. It was marvelous to see! Some gave their lives to the Lord Jesus Christ. All because the glory of God stepped up into the room, took over and made it His own, as He showed me in the Spirit of the vision of His throne coming down into the room! To see the Spirit of God move so mightily in that room that night in the way that He did was a blessing to witness. To see the Spirit of the Lord move in and on souls that were hungry for Him and what He was giving them was just amazing to behold and I felt blessed and honored to witness and be a part of it! Words cannot explain the joy I felt that night at what the Lord was doing for all those that were in the room and for my soul as well in that place that night. The blessing was mine! The Lord taught me that His Spirit can shine anywhere and on anyone and at any time! We all have some sort of prison at sometime in our lives that we have needed to be delivered from whether it is mental, physical, or emotional, we all have had or have prisons that have at sometime in our life has held us captive, but God! Christ said He came to set the captives free;

The Spirit of the Lord is upon me, because he hath anointed me to preach the gospel to the poor; He hath sent me to heal the broken-hearted, to preach deliverance to the captives, and recovering of sight to the blind, to set at liberty them that are bruised, - Luke 4: 18, KJV)

We were then asked if we wouldn't mind praying for others outside of the room, we agreed and were lead to go out to the courtyard were there were others sitting at tables and doing various recreations who had not come to the meeting, and where asked to pray for them as well. The authorities allowed it and we went forth. Once again the Spirit of the Lord met us there as well! Those who had been blessed by God in the meeting were telling the others to come and hear what the Lord was saying through those who had come to pray and hold Bible study that night! Many gathered around the table outside in the court yard to hear and be prayed for, it was amazing! My heart was so full of the gladness of the Lord to see so many eager to hear the word of the Lord and to be prayed for, I could hardly contain myself. When the Lord finally released us to go, we were asked by the administration if we would also pray for them before we left, we agreed. They said that they had heard what had gone on in the meeting. They told us how that the women were coming up to them excited and telling them and that they should come and hear and see what the Lord was doing in the room through prayer and how God was moving in the room! Talk about a Holy Ghost fire that yet continued to burn! The spirit of the Lord Jesus stepped up in the room that night and went to work! Setting His throne in the midst and turned it into His own! I gave my testimony of being in a prison in my mind for eighteen years, and how that when I thought I had left one mental prison, Satan just gave me another, locking me up inside until I despaired of life itself. Then one day I met Jesus in the door of the courtyard of my prison of the soul and mind and He showed me another side, outside of the walls of my prison, a place of freedom, freedom from bondages, hindrances, confusions, demoniac influences and manipulations, freedom from being bound always to the consequences of sin and the weakness and choices of my flesh. Where freedom reigned in my soul no matter what my situation, and He set me free! Satan's chains could no longer hold me, I was set free! And free indeed! All because of Christ! I told them that this prison of brick and mortar was nothing compared to being imprisoned in the mind and their spirit, locked up inside and unable to break yourself free, but how that with Christ, we can do all things and it is He who sets us free and it is the power of the Holy Ghost that keeps us free. I told them that in the material prison once they had served their sentence they were able to walk out of it free. But the prison of the mind you just can't walk out of, it takes Jesus to get you out! And if you believed on Him, turned to Him and repented of your sins, He would get you out and you would be out for good! To be free in your mind, soul and spirit, there is no greater freedom! That's a freedom that no man can take away from you once you have received it! Not only would He set you free inside of these prison walls but when you are released from these prison walls, you would stay free outside of these walls as well. You can have the better life in Christ Jesus our Lord and Savior! It is the choices that we make that determines or decides what prisons we make for ourselves, but it is the Lord's good will to set us free from whatever prison the enemy has made us captive. As long as you put your trust in Jesus and follow Him! He will never leave you nor forsake you! How did I know, because I tried Him for myself and every day that I wake up, I fight for my freedom by keeping my mind focused on Christ Jesus, because it is a fight as long as there is a devil in this world, it will be a fight. It is a fight already won though in Christ for all those who believe on His name. These words were like apples of gold in pictures of silver for many that night and not only blessed those that received them, but also blessed the ones who were giving them! To God, be all the Glory! Amen!

The Gift of Flowers

"Consider the lilies how they grow; they toil not, they spin not; and yet I say unto you, that Solomon in all his glory was not arrayed like one of these." – (Luke 12: 27, KJV)

"Flowers appear on the earth; the season of singing has come, the cooing of doves is heard in our land."– (Song of Solomon 2: 12, NIV)

"Finally, brethren, whatsoever things are true, whatsoever things are honest, whatsoever things are just, whatsoever things are pure, whatsoever things are lovely, whatsoever things are of good report; if there be any virtue, and if there be any praise, think on these things." – (Philippians 4: 8, KJV)

One of things I have come to love about the Lord God and my Savior Jesus Christ is that they love making things beautiful. You can tell it when you look at nature, the universe, the stars and planets, as well as all the different ethnicities among the people here on this earth, there is beauty everywhere. To be simply put, God loves beautiful things. Flowers are said to symbolize, rebirth or new birth, new beginnings and eternal life, soul and virtue. It is no wonder why God included so many in His creation of this world and placed them all over this earth, just like man. Some type of flower can be found blooming in some of the most arid of terrains. Areas where you would normally think a flower should not grow, there is where you may find one of God's beautiful creations not only growing, but thriving as well. Some flowers are said to symbolize love, as well as the blood of Jesus, like the red rose. They are also said to express divine goodness, truth and beauty. The white lily is said to express Christ's purity and divinity and hope along with symbolizing resurrection. The daffodil is said to represent eternal life in Christ and rebirth. Tulips are said to symbolize forgiveness. Easter lilies symbolize virtue, innocence, life as well as eternal life in heaven. Azaleas are said to represent temperance or self control, with various colors of it representing different things. Daises are said to represent loyalty, and gentleness. Baby's breath are said to symbolize the presence of the Holy Spirit. Iris's are said to express faith, wisdom and hope. Hyacinths are said to convey a message of peace of mind. The pink carnation is said to represent remembrance. Flowers of blue represent hope, flowers of purple for royalty. Whatever the flower or its color, God has a purpose for its being and I believe all are just another expression of God's divinity, His love and hope for all mankind, as well as the life we are to live with Him, now and in the future as well as the eternal, God's gift of flowers.

✢ Testimonies of the Heart:

I've always loves flowers their colors, their sent and all their many varieties, of course I had my favorites, but as a hold, I truly love them all. One day while riding on the bus on my way into work, some years ago, when I worked in nursing, I was looking out the window as I found myself often doing while riding down the road. I found myself wishing that I had some flowers. In fact, I was wishing that someone would give me some flowers, (smile). Now at the time I knew of no one who could do that or would be willing to do that, but, after all it was just a wish or so I thought. Putting it out of my mind I went to work, not thinking about it again. Upon catching the bus after work back into downtown, I decided I would take a walk down Main street as I sometimes did when I felt that I had time to do so and would just look around. I liked going to the Peanut shop where they roasted the various nuts right there before you. The smell of the roasted nuts would go all through downtown and brought many customers in to buy them. While walking in front of the main office plaza, I saw a person walking with a big basket of flowers. They were beautiful! I couldn't help but compliment her on the beautiful basket as she got closer to me. They seemed to be a little upset. They stopped when I complimented them on the basket and said, "Do you think so?" I said, "Yes!" and that, they were absolutely gorgeous, thinking that someone who liked her very much had given her the beautiful bouquet, I was not quite in understanding of her frustration at the time. They went on to tell me that they were a florist and that they owned a floral shop down town. I told them, I knew the shop, and that the flower bouquets that were in the windows were just beautiful. They thanked me for my compliments and said that they had made the bouquet for a executive who worked in a bank for a present for his wife. The man had told them the flowers that he wanted in the bouquet and to make it big. So they did and had stayed after hours in their shop after closing to take their time to make the arraignment as lovely as they could make it, considering it was going to be a gift for the customer's wedding anniversary to their wife. They went on further to say that they decided to deliver the flowers their self since they were going to an executive in the bank. They then went on to tell me the cost of the floral arraignment needless to say it was very expensive! After they had painstakingly took the time to put the floral arraignment together instead of having one of their shop workers do it, and took it up to the customer, the executive took one look at it and said he did not like it, and to take it back and make another one! Now of course they were not happy with the man's adamant statement to take the flowers back and make him another bouquet, especially after all the time they took to make that it and personally deliver it them self. I sympathized with them, because the flowers were absolutely beautiful and the way that they had been arraigned showed the effort and the time staking ability that they had put in to making it. I told them that I was sorry to hear about what the man said and his rejection of the flowers, because they were just gorgeous! As we both turned to go our own separate directions, I heard them call out to me, "Miss, do you like these flowers?" Again I said yes. They told me that when she got back to the shop they were just going to be thrown away because they don't use the flowers twice once they have already been placed in a bouquet and they were just going to make another arraignment for the customer any way. I stood there wondering, what were, they trying to say, they then asked if I wanted the flowers, I was stunned! Immediately, I said "Yes!" But I didn't have the money on me to pay for them. They then went on further to say that they were free, and that I did not have to pay anything for them. They said that they were already paid for and again, all they were going to do was make another one and that they didn't want throw the bouquet away because they had took so much time in making it. They said they would rather give them to someone who would appreciate them and love them as they did once they saw how beautiful the arraignment had turned out. I started crying, because no one had ever done anything like that for me before. They pulled me out a tissue and placed it in my hands and then placed this big beautiful and absolutely expensive, gorgeous bouquet put together with all of my most favorite flowers in my hands! There were purple Iris's, yellow daffodils, pink carnations, white Baby's breath, colorful Daises, red carnations, pink and white closed bud roses, bright orange lilies, colorful tulips and so on. They smiled and told me to be blessed, and turned and walked away not once looking back! I on the other hand, for a few moments, could not move. I was so stunned and surprised until I was just speechless. I knew that this was Jesus! He heard my wish, my heart's desire, spoken in my spirit without an idea of ever being answered, or having made a request for! It was just a wish, a silent heart's desire, thought of and then quickly dismissed as never going to happen, yet heard by the Lord. I know many times we may think that the Lord does not hear even our faintest desire of our hearts, but He does and if you will trust Him and follow Him, He will prove it to you. We serve a caring God, not a God that is far away and does not hear the desires of our heart. He hears, He cares, and He answers! I shared my testimony with the church that night at Bible study and brought in the flowers as a witness of God's goodness toward His people to show to everybody how that when we think He doesn't hear, God hears even the simplest of desires of the heart. A gift of flowers! Many in service that night were surprised as well, that the Lord would answer what was not even asked of Him. The kindness and the thoughtfulness of God of that shown in the gift left many encouraged and joyful along with me. It reminded me of a verse in - Psalm 34:4, KJV;

Delight thyself also in the LORD and He shall give thee the desires of thine heart. –(Psalm 37: 4, KJV).

Some admitted to me after church that they had never thought about the Lord in that way as to answer a desire of the heart that was not even prayed for. They like I did at the time, did not look at just how much God cares for us to take note or pay attention to these things that we consider small, but this experience showed me just how much God is looking at the desires of our heart, even when we don't think He cares, He constantly proves He does. It opened up a whole new view of our Lord that I had not seen before, and in so doing allowed me to share it with others to see the depth of the love of our Lord for His people in a whole new light. Jesus truly is the bridegroom of the church and He loves His Bride and the Bride loves their groom, King Jesus! Does not the groom sometimes in thinking of the bride give His bride the gift of flowers? I say, yes and amen.

Consider the lilies of the field, how they grow; they toil not, neither do they spin:

And yet I say unto you, That Solomon in all his glory was not arrayed like one of these. - (Matthew 6:28, 29, KJV)

A BREATH OF FRESH AIR

So Jesus came again into Cana of Galilee, the Galileans received him, having seen all the things that He did at Jerusalem at the feast: for they also went unto the feast.

So Jesus came again into Cana of Galilee, where He made the water wine. And there was a certain nobleman, whose son was sick at Capernaum.

When He heard that Jesus was come out of Judaea into Galilee, he went unto Him, and besought Him that He would come down, and heal his son: for he was at the point of death.

Then said Jesus unto him, Except ye see signs and wonders, ye will not believe.

The nobleman saith unto Him, Sir; come down ere my child die.

Jesus saith unto him, Go thy way; thy son liveth. And the man believed the word that Jesus had spoken unto him, and he went his way. – (John 4: 45 – 50, KJV)

Now the miracle that Christ had done at the wedding feast was still in the mind of the nobleman who had also attended the same wedding feast the first time Jesus and His disciples had come to Cana. Knowing that Christ had the power to do miracles and no doubt having possibly heard of other miracles that Christ had performed since, asked Christ to come and heal his son. Christ put the nobleman's faith in Him to heal his son to the test. He told him that unless he saw a sign or a wonder he would not believe. This had to make the nobleman think about, what Christ had said. What was He saying, unless I see it happen, I will not believe it to happen? So the nobleman answered no doubt after pondering what Jesus had said, and again asked him to come down and heal his son. Jesus told him, to go his way, his son lives. Right there and then, his mind cleared, and he understood it was a test of his faith! The next thing you read is that the man believed the word that Jesus had spoken and went his way. His faith increased! Jesus challenged him to believe for what he could not see and that He could heal his son without him having to see Him do it. That was a true test of faith. We read in the verses that follow that indeed the man's son was healed and at the very hour Jesus spoke it. This in turn led to the whole nobleman's house believing in Christ Jesus because of this one act of faith for believing without seeing! What a challenge, here you are in another city a ways from home not knowing of what your child's condition might be, but on a word from the Lord, you take faith, grab unto belief without sight, not really knowing but believing anyway, and Jesus answers your request! How wonderful is that?! The people of the city of Nazareth missed their blessing because of unbelief, but the people of Cana grabbed hold to theirs and because of their belief, were blessed because of their faith in Jesus Christ!

✦ TESTIMONIES OF THE HEART:

Back some years ago when my son was ten, he had asthma. He had it so bad until he couldn't even walk up a few steps without giving out of wind. I had to watch my child to sit down on the steps and try to take deep breaths just to breathe, even with an inhaler. My heart grieved for him, I was scared my boy was not going to be able to catch a breath one day and was going die from an asthma attack. I asked the pastor if he would pray for him. He said to me, if I had faith to believe that Jesus could heal my son of asthma, Jesus would heal him. I must admit at that time I had never seen anyone get healed of asthma before in my life and my faith was a little shaky where as this was concerned. I had nothing to go on as far as witness or testimony. Nevertheless I knew that Jesus was a healer and I had seen the Spirit of the Lord work in the midst of prayer during altar call on others, so I knew He could if He wanted too. So the challenge came to my faith in Jesus to do it for my boy. I was nervous at first that my faith might not be enough for the Lord to heal my son, but I said yes any way, and that I believed that Jesus could heal my son. I was determined, because I wanted my son to be able to breathe normally without worrying when he might not be able to catch a breath, I was afraid that one of these times he might not be able to get to his inhaler in time and breath, I did not want to see my son die from an asthma attack that was not caught in time. I grabbed hold and took and allowed the Lord to stretch my faith. I was determined I was going to go up to the altar with him and stand with him in support of him the next church service day. That following Sunday the pastor called my son up to the altar, I came with him. He asked him did he want to breathe normal again, my son said yes. While the pastor was talking to him, I stood behind my son praying and asking the Lord Jesus Christ to increase my faith for a miracle for my son to be healed of asthma. He then asked him if he believed that Jesus could heal him. My son said in that child like faith that believes without question or doubt, so many of us are missing these days, that faith that doesn't have to see to believe, "Yes". My pastor prayed for him calling on the name of Jesus, and in the name of Jesus, my son was healed of asthma once and for all, Hallelujah! My son is now grown and has a family with children of his own and has never once suffered with asthma since that prayer, one Sunday morning, over 31 years ago. It doesn't matter if you have never seen a miracle being performed before your eyes, if you have that child like faith to believe in what you cannot see God do, but can have faith and trust in Him regardless, to do, know that God can and God will do it for you. That one miracle increased my faith for many more miracles to happen in my life and are still happening in my life. I didn't understand why pastor asked me that at first. No doubt the Spirit of the Lord may have revealed to him the shakiness in my spirit concerning the level of faith that I had at the time, I don't know, but I am glad he did. Because like the nobleman that was challenged by Jesus to believe without him having to see Jesus physically laying hands on his son healing him of the sickness. I had to believe Jesus was going to heal my son even though I had not seen anyone healed of his sickness before, and thank God I did! From this experience, I have learned you don't have to see faith working for it to work! It is the power of God that goes to work through your faith. My son's child like faith, combined with my newly increased faith, moved the heart of God to work in my son's favor, to heal him completely of asthma, all for a breath of fresh air. Glory to God!! My son's childlike faith to believe God without question that day caused me to step into a greater faith in God and trust and belief in Him, not just in healing but in all things! Thank you Lord Jesus!

Suffer little children to come unto me, and forbid them not: for of such is the kingdom of God. – (Luke 18: 16, KJV)

MERCY AND
THE ANGEL

Come unto Me, all ye that labour and are heavy laden, and I will give you rest.

Take My yoke upon you, and learn of Me; for I am meek and lowly of heart: and ye shall find rest unto your souls.

For My yoke is easy, and My burden is light." – (Matthew 11: 28-30, KJV)

"But when Jesus heard that, He said unto them, They that be whole need not a physician, but they that are sick.

But go ye and learn what that meaneth, I will have mercy, and not sacrifice: for I am not come to call the righteous, but sinners to repentance." – (Matthew 9: 12, 13, KJV)

"And as Jesus passed forth from thence, He saw a man, named Matthew, sitting at the receipt of custom: and saith unto him, Follow me. And he arose, and followed Him. – (Matthew 9: 9, KJV)

Many times Christ faced skeptics and self righteous Pharisees when it came to His forgiveness of sinners, but He did not let that stop Him from forgiving all those who came to Him. Jesus understood that those who came to Him needed His help and His forgiveness of their sins. The self righteous Pharisees and scribes that often confronted Jesus never recognized their sins as well as their need to be forgiven. They thought that since they held the religious positions that they did that it meant that they were already righteous, but Christ proved that to the contrary. Jesus provided rest from the burdens and the yoke of a sin laden life, whose consequences are too much to bear at times. He spoke about the labor of sin, meaning the life that we live apart from God and how that it causes us to be heavy laden, in other words weighted down with burdens, problems and distresses of the mind, will, and spirit causing us to be bowed down with the results of our own iniquities. Christ bids us to come to Him and He will give us rest. He then begins to show the difference between following Him and following the adversary. Jesus' burdens are light in that Christ gives us victory over sin and its consequences, but the yokes and the burdens of the enemy are to break you and bring into a slave demeanor, whereas the Lord would have us to serve one another out of love not esteeming one above another. The enemy gives us no choice all his ways lead to destruction and the tearing down of the will, the mind and the body and soul. In Christ Jesus all our labors are to the building up of mind, body, soul and spirit the direct opposite of Satan and his plans for our demise or end. The enemy of our souls is a hard task master, stripping us all resemblance of who God created us to be. God created us in His image, a reflection of Himself, righteous and holy. Satan is out to destroy any image or reflection of that in our souls and in our life. By his constant attack upon our minds and our will, when we submit to his will and to his pressure to sin, it weakens our resolve and we become bowed over, or burdened with the results and the consequences of our actions and decisions, but thank God, we don't have to stay that way. Jesus is freedom! And when we repent of our sins and accept Him as Lord and Savior in our lives, we can become set free. Then there are times Christ comes to us when He sees that we are too entangled to come to Him, just as Matthew was when Jesus saw him and came to him;

And as Jesus passed forth from thence, He saw a man, named Matthew, sitting at the receipt of custom: and He saith unto him, Follow me. And he arose, and followed Him. - (Matthew 9: 9, KJV)

I believe in Matthew probably was seeking a better life, but like so many of us, sometimes we need help to find our way to Christ Jesus our Lord and Savior. He may have known that this was not the life he wanted to live, but his circumstances and his choice had brought him to that place, that if Christ had not come to him that day, who knows if Matthew would have ever found his way. Sometimes in life we get stuck in a rut and it takes Jesus to get us out! Most of Christ's disciples were caught up in other lives before they knew Christ as Lord and Savior and Christ had to come and find them, and find them He did and called them into freedom and His glorious light, by just two powerful words, "Follow me.;

And He saith unto them, Follow me, and I will make you fishers of men. – Matthew 4:19, KJV)

He knew that if he did not reach out to them, they might not have come to Him, not knowing Him and who he was. They might have missed their chance at salvation, but mercy found them and saved them.

⤳ Testimonies of the Heart:

Back before I became saved and born again, I was going through some very intense struggles dealing with abuse and violence, and mental anguish that tormented and stressed my mind and soul on a daily basis. It had become just too terrible for me to continue to bear. Distraught over what my life had become, I found myself contemplating taking my life. One night while on my knees at the foot of my bed, I started praying. Not really knowing how to pray, I just started talking, hoping that someone was listening. I didn't know God, I knew of Him, and I didn't have a relationship with Jesus, but I kept praying any way, I didn't even know if anyone was listening, I just hoped. Things were bad I became more and more discouraged and disheartened. I had a friend I hadn't talked to in a while it was like they just disappeared. I found out later that they had got back into church and had rededicated their life back to the Lord. That was a part of my talk to the Lord that night at the foot of my bed, as I was praying about everything under the sun to God, not knowing if He heard me or even if He was listening to my prayer. My friend had once been in the church, something that I admired about her and her relationship with the God I did not know. Even though my life wasn't so, I had become very much grieved when I heard that they had left the church.

When I found out that they had got back into church, I begged them to tell me what church they were going to. I knew for them to be drawn back into the house of God, there had to be something pretty powerful going on, considering what kind of church they used to go to. I called their house and was given the number of the church they were attending, I was desperate. I had decided that if I did not get help for myself, I was going to end mu life that night. I took a chance on them being there and called, thank God, they were. I asked them to please come and get me, that I wanted to come to church, they agreed. With my one year old son in my arms and my three year old daughter at my side, I gathered them up and went to church. As service progressed and it came prayer time, I watched as everyone went down on their knees to pray. I was so distraught in my soul and my mind, I couldn't pray. I got up off my knees and said within myself, hurt that nothing seemed to be working, plus there is the fact, I really didn't know at the time what I was doing. Once again, I told myself, If I didn't get any help tonight I was going home and call my parents to come and get my children and I was going to take my life. I sat there in the back of the church just miserable. I looked out over the sanctuary and everything seemed to be glowing. I didn't understand. Service ended and I was waiting on my friend to take me home, having settled in my mind what I was going to do. All of a sudden, I heard a voice telling me to get up and go to the front. I looked around to see who was talking to me. Having seen no one, I ignored the voice. It came again, "Get up and go to the front and talk to the man that was sitting up front!" This time it scared me, because it came even firmer than before. Being quite ignorant of the voice of the Lord, I thought the church had ghosts! I know it sounds funny, but that was my thinking at the time, I didn't know the voice of the Lord then, I just knew that something or someone was calling me to go up front. I began to argue in my mind, seeing as to how I heard this voice speaking to me clearly in my mind and it wasn't me! I argued with it that I wasn't going up there. I didn't know the man up front and I didn't want him to think I was crazy. I told the voice, I'm not going up there, still thinking about what I was going to do when I got home. All of a sudden I felt two hands strongly pull me out of the seat, while I was still holding my son! It felt like two arms just wrapped around my body holding me hostage, and walked me up front and then after walking me up front, and firmly sat me down on the seat. Again I heard the voice more sternly say and even louder in my head, "Talk to the man up front!" By this time I was truly scared, seeing no one strong arm me and bring me up front, but yet I felt it every bit of it and I knew something or someone, who I could not see, dragged me holding my son more like a security than me protecting him, up front. Too scared to disappoint who ever "It" was that dragged me up front, I waited until I got the attention of the man up front. The man up front was the pastor of the church, after starring at him intently for minutes as he talked with the other members, I was too scared to speak. Not fully understanding what was going on at the time I really did not know what else to do, but stare. Finally he recognized me starring at him and asked if everything was alright? I asked him if I could speak to him privately. He said yes, and we went to his office. He asked me, "How could he help me?" Still very nervous, I told him, I didn't know what the people that were down in the sanctuary had, but whatever they had, I wanted it. He told me that all they had was Jesus. I said "Okay", and then asked him, how do I get Him? Well, Praises be to the God of glory and my Savior Jesus Christ, I became saved and born again and filled with the Holy Ghost the same night. My life has been changed ever since! Instead of going home with a mind to die, I went home with a mind to live! I know now that the invisible hands and the arms that I felt pull me out of my seat while holding me firmly, walking me to the front of the church, setting me and my son down on the front row in front of the Pastor, had to have been one of God's angels. The Lord knew that if He did not come to me that night my life and my soul would have been lost and in Hell I would have lifted up my eyes. I know now that Mercy came and got me that night, just like He did so many years ago those disciples that did not know Him, but yet needed him so badly and His deep compassion and loving desire for all mankind to be saved. This leads me to share my heart's desire, and that is, once the Lord Jesus comes to you, don't turn Him away. You don't know whose life as well as soul, you might be saving along with your own. It was the mercy of Jesus Christ that came to me to save my life as well as my soul and it was His mercy that sent the angel to pull me and my child out of the seat that night during one of the darkest hours of my life, and then to wrap me up in his arms and take me to the front of the church and sit me down, pulling me all the way from the back of the church, and thank God He did, I am saved today and able to tell the story. To God, be all the Glory!! Mercy and the Angel.

Because he hath set His love upon Me, therefore will I deliver him: I will set him on high, because he hath known My name.

He shall call upon Me, and I will answer him: I will be with Him in trouble; I will deliver him, and honour him.

With long life will I satisfy him, and shew him My salvation. – (Psalm 91: 14-16, KJV)

THE UNEXPECTED MIRACLE

And when He was departed thence, He went into their synagogue:

And behold, there was a man which had his hand withered. And they asked him, saying, Is it lawful to heal on the Sabbath days? that they might accuse him.

And he said unto them, What man shall there be among you, that shall have one sheep, and if it fall into a pit on the Sabbath day, will he not lay hold on it, and lift it out?

How much then is a man better than a sheep? Wherefore it is lawful to do well on the Sabbath days.

Then saith He to the man, Stretch forth thine hand. And he stretched it forth; and it was restored whole, like as the other. – (Matthew 12: 9- 13, KJV)

And He said unto them, The sabbath was made for man, and not man for the Sabbath:

Therefore the Son of man is Lord also of the Sabbath. – (Mark 2: 27, 28, KJV)

The Sabbath is a day of rest given unto man by God to rest from his labors and to worship the Lord. It is commanded by God to be observed, just as God rested from all His work in creation, so He commanded man also to observe a day of rest. I can just imagine that the man when he went into the synagogue that day never expected that he would not leave out, the same way he came in. No doubt the man was thinking that this would be just another Sabbath just like the ones before when he would go into the synagogue to worship the Lord, but this time it was different, Jesus was there! This unexpected miracle of rest from an affliction which withered this man's hand and more than likely caused him no end of physical duress along with the forgiveness of his sins, sins which brought no peace to his soul, was no doubt received with much gladness of heart, soul and spirit. Many Jewish leaders and people of that day associated sickness and afflictions with the committing of sin. They thought that if you had or were suffering from some sort of affliction of the body, that you must have committed a sin worthy of the judgment of the affliction. Just as Job's friends thought concerning Job, which we learned from the beginning of the book of Job was as far from the truth as one could get. Jesus knowing the misguided thoughts of the leaders of the synagogue concerning the man's affliction, first forgave the man of his sins then proceeded to heal him, proving that He was Lord of the Sabbath and able to not only to give rest to the body because of sickness, but also peace to the soul because of sins. Talk about being in the right place at the right time! What a wonderful day it was for the man whose withered hand was healed and his sins forgiven! He may have come into the synagogue expecting just another service that day thinking that it was just another Sabbath that he had attended many times before and nothing had changed, until he met Jesus, and an unexpected miracle of peace and rest for his body and his soul was given him! It truly became a day of rest for this wearied soul and an unexpected miracle! Hallelujah!

⇢ Testimonies of the Heart:

In the year 2000, I had received a word from the Lord that in five years He was going to heal me of the sickness that I was suffering with and He was going to heal me before the world. Having seen and been to many doctors over the years concerning it and being told I would die with it because there was no cure for it. I received the word with anticipation. As the years began to go by and I began increasingly more to suffer because of the sickness that seemed to have my body captive, my hope began to wane and more and more, I found myself becoming acceptable of the thought that I might never be healed of the affliction and I forgot about the word that was given me by the Holy Spirit. I began to live my life, that, never the less what was going on in my health that I was going to serve the Lord with all my heart, mind, and soul anyway and try to do with the best of my ability whatever the Holy Spirit laid in my spirit to do. I had started a prayer ban and Bible Study group in my home, as the prayer and bible study grew and many different ones began to come, it opened up opportunities for me to visit many different churches as well as a guest of the different ones who attended my prayer and bible study meetings. On one such occasion I learned that the church of one of the ministers that attended my prayer and bible study meeting would be traveling to a Benny Hinn prayer meeting in Detroit,

Michigan. The minister invited me to come along with them and that they were going in hopes of being healed of the troubles that she was going through in her body due unto an accident she had been in sometime before. I agreed and went along to support them praying that complete healing and not expecting anything for myself. As I stated earlier, my hope had waned, I had all but given into the mind of not ever being healed and just living my life with the affliction, but I was not going to let that stop me from praying for others. When we arrived in Detroit the meeting was being held in the Joe Louis Arena, it was packed! Having never been to a professional sports arena, I didn't know it was so big inside. Every seat was taken except for areas that had been reserved for churches that had made their reservations in advance. As we found the area that was reserved for us, we sat down. As the service was going forth, I started to have a flare up of the sickness that was going on in my body. Intense pain, swelling and muscle weakness took me over. My whole body was starting to go limp and pain and nerve sensitivity was increasingly exponentially quickly. I started to panic. I didn't know what to do. I knew I would not be able to get out of the stadium without help and there was a possibility of falling down and going unconscious or someone having to literally hold me up and drag me along because of the limpness in my muscles hindering my ability to walk on my own. Getting in the van that brought us there and taking the long trip back home was out of the question, I knew I would not make it. I told them, that I might not be able to make it out of the arena and that they might have to take me to a hotel and leave me there and I would take the greyhound bus back home in the morning hopefully after the flare up had passed. Seeing the worried look on my face, they told me to just start praying! I was sitting there asking God to heal them when the attack happened to me. I started praying asking the Lord to please stop the pain and to strengthen my muscles so I could walk out of the stadium and make the long trip back home.

As prayer worship and prayer was going forth in the stadium, I began to feel a tingling go all over my body and the pain I was suffering ceased and I felt my muscles regain strength, the weakness in my body left. Excited I turned to my friend and told her that the pain was gone and I was strong again! Happy that I would be able to go back with them in the van that night home, I started praising God right there in my seat just glad that the pain was gone and I had the control over my limbs again. They started a testimonial line in the arena for all those who had received something done unto them by the Lord to come up before Benny Hinn to give their testimony. They told me I should get in the line, I told them no, and that there was no way and that there was too many people there and I was too scared to go before all those people, she kept trying, and I kept turning her down. Finally they stopped trying to get me to go. I was glad they left me alone. Then all of a sudden my hips turned and my legs started walking out of the row where we were sitting and down towards the arena floor!! They asked me, "Where are you going!" I said I didn't know! I did not have the control of my body! And that something was moving my legs and body and it wasn't me! They said what? I shouted back as Spirit had hold of me, literally and physically, leading me down the steps to the floor of the arena, "I guess God wants me to get in the line!" and tell my testimony anyway! If you have never experienced this in the Lord before, it is a scary thing! To not to have the control of your limbs and they start walking all of a sudden by their selves while carrying you along! I understood that it was the Lord's will for me to do this and that I had to get over my stage fright in a hurry, because I was about to be put out in front of what looked like thousands of people whether I wanted to or not!! Yeah, it was like that! When I made it downstairs and got in line the hold that was on my legs and body went away. I knew it was for me to stay there. I was so nervous, I just closed my eyes and just started praying for the Lord to give me courage to stay there and to take the fear of being called up to stand in front of all those people out of me. No one knew that I suffered with stage fright, because when they saw or witnessed me go forth in church and other places, all they saw was the confidence of the Lord. They didn't know the battle I faced every time within me, to get there and how it took the Spirit of the Lord to encourage me and to come in and take over to do what they witnessed the Lord do through me. It was something I suffered with all through childhood and into adulthood, but when I got saved, I was determined I was not going to let it stop me, even if I had to do battle. I constantly prayed for Holy Ghost boldness before I went forth in anything that involved me going before many.

As I stood in line wondering what was going to happen next, I saw many, many people being healed and delivered all around me! I had never seen healing on this scale before or witnessed the power of God working so massively like I witnessed the Spirit of the Lord working that day! It was just indescribable! I started bouncing around from foot to foot, watching everything that was going on, not knowing what to do. I started thinking all I had to report was that the pain had stopped, but never the less I knew I could not leave the line! As we drew closer to the stage and I saw the wonders of the Spirit of the Lord increase, so did the stage fright I was suffering with increase as well. I was now trying to physically hide from sight behind others standing in front of me. As I watched many become slain in the Spirit, I didn't want it to be me, not in front of all those people! So I hid until I could not hide anymore! Before I was called up on stage, I was asked by one of the ministers that were questioning those of us in line, "What had the Lord done for me?" I replied that He took all my pain away. I was then asked what was wrong with me and how long had I suffered with it, and had I been to the doctor about it? I told him of the sickness that I had and how long I had suffered with it and how that I had seen many doctors concerning it to no avail. I still had no clue that what happened next, was going to happen. I thought I was just going to give my testimony about the pain going away and that would be that and then proceed to get off the stage. When they brought me before Benny and told him what I had and how long I had suffered with it, and how I had seen many doctors to no avail, He took one look at me and without question or comment, immediately in the name of Jesus commanded the spirit of sickness to come out of me! I looked at him and saw this really bright ball of light like a ball of lightning come down from above over his head and go in him, travel down his arm out of his hand and just burst in front of me!! I felt something bodily just tear away from my body! The force of it just literally snapped my head around I immediately fell to the floor! Even though I know I hit it hard, but I felt nothing! All the strength in me was gone, all I could do was lay there, healed! Later he had someone to pick me up. They did, my whole body was weak, like someone who had been drinking, a lot! It is what we call in the church being "drunk in the Spirit" it is where you are so overwhelmed by the power of God until there is no strength left in you. He spoke a word of God over me and I went out again. This time when they picked me up, again I was so drunk in the Spirit until I literally staggered off the stage, totally delivered! This was in the year 2005, exactly five years from the year that the Holy Spirit told me, I would be healed and just like He said it was before the world! Benny Hinn, a powerful and anointed man of God, healing prayer meetings at that time were being broadcast all over the world and there I was, as the Lord had revealed to me five years before being healed before the world. This indeed was an unexpected miracle for me, because of the intensity of what I was going through, I had lost hope, and forgot about what the Spirit of the Lord had promised me five years before, but God did not forget me. God remembered me, and despite my lack of hope and faith in Him to do what He said, He did it anyway, and I thank and love Him for it and I thank Him for it every time I think about the unexpected miracle that He performed for me that day while praying for another. It taught me to never give up hope on the promises of God no matter how long they take to come to pass. God will do just as He says! Thank you Lord Jesus! For even when we forget, and do not remember the word that was spoken by your Holy Spirit unto us and your promises unto us, you do not forget us nor do you forget your word and your promises to your children. Praises be to God!!

He hath remembered His mercy and His truth toward the house of Israel: all the ends of earth have seen the salvation of our God. – (Psalm 98: 3, KJV)

SPEAK THE WORD

And when Jesus was entered into Capernaum, there came unto Him a centurion, beseeching Him,

And saying, Lord, my servant lieth at home sick of the palsy, grievously tormented.

And Jesus saith unto him, I will come and heal him.

The centurion answered and said, Lord, I am not worthy that Thou shouldest come under my roof: but speak the word only, and my servant shall be healed.

When Jesus heard it, He marveled, and said to them that followed, Verily I say unto you, I have not found so great faith, no, not in Israel.

And Jesus said unto the centurion, Go thy way; and as thou hast believed, so be it done unto thee. And his servant was healed in the selfsame hour.

When the even was come, they brought unto Him many that were possessed with devils: and He cast out the spirits with His word, and healed the sick: - (Matthew 8: 5-8, 10, 13, 16, KJV)

The word of Jesus Christ has power! The centurion no doubt having heard of Christ and how he healed people sent for Him;

And when he heard of Jesus, he sent unto Him the elders of the Jews, beseeching Him that He would come and heal his servant. – (Luke 7: 3, KJV)

The centurion just from hearing about Christ took faith and believed Him for the word that he heard. There were many in that day that Jesus did not have to lay hands on to heal them, but instead just spoke the word and they were healed. God's word carries God's promise and God's power! The centurion was a Roman and not a Jew he was not raised in the knowledge of God. But having lived among them he had come to love them and as Luke 7:5, (KJV);

For he loveth our nation, and he hath built us a synagogue. – (Luke 7:5, KJV)

) tells us, he even built them a synagogue to worship God in. So honored was he because of his love for the Jewish people and their nation, that the Jewish people loved him back and counted him worthy of his request of Jesus being a Jew, for the healing of his servant. I believe what touched the heart of Christ so, was the faith that the Roman centurion being not a Jew, had in Him to believe for the healing of his servant without Jesus having to come and lay hands on him in order for him to be healed, but speak the word. The centurion understood that Christ had the power of God in him and that He had the authority to direct that power wherever and whenever he pleased.

For I also am a man set under authority, having under me soldiers, and I say unto one, Go, and he goeth; and to another, Come, and he cometh; and to my servant, Do this and he doeth it. - (Luke 7: 8, KJV)

Christ did not have to travel to the man's house the faith of the centurion reached out and told Christ but speak the word and his servant would be healed;

Wherefore neither thought I myself worthy to come unto thee: but say in word, and my servant shall be healed. - (Luke 7:7, KJV)

When God speaks, neither distance or time matters, because God's word is eternal it exists out of time and space. It has no boundaries and it has no limits, it is only to be believed, have faith in and trusted, for the promise, the power and the presence of God that it carries!

✦ TESTIMONIES OF THE HEART:

Back when I was seven years old my father passed away. My mother had remarried by then and we were living in the state. My mother shared with us that my father had died of cancer. Later on in years she told me just how bad the cancer was that caused his death. I often thought about this whenever it was mentioned about someone being sick with cancer. When I was saved, one of my main prayers to God was to please not let me die of cancer like my father did. One day while praying about this to the Lord and making my request known unto Him, I heard the voice of the Lord reply back to me, "No cancer would touch my body." I immediately accepted the word of God spoken to me by the Holy Spirit. Thankful and grateful, I believed Him at His word. Some years later, Cysts developed in both of my breasts. I had been taking these weight loss pills, I had seen advertised a lot on TV and being unnecessarily burdened and concerned about my weight, I bought them and started taking them trying to lose some weight. Unfortunately they had an adverse affect they caused cysts to grow in my breasts. There was an ingredient in the pills that was causing the problem. I stopped taking them when I found out, but the cysts had already formed. I went to the doctor who then sent me to a specialist, and every so often I would have to go in to have them aspirated, meaning to have the fluid withdrawn out of them, a very painful process indeed. I went into prayer about what was going on in my body. While in prayer, I heard the Spirit of the Lord tell me to go back to my doctor and tell them, these words, that the Lord said, to remove the cysts from my breasts before they caused me problems. Now I knew that this was not going to be readily accepted by them, to go in there and tell them that the Lord said, but never the less, I was obedient unto the Spirit of the Lord. I made the appointment, went in and boldly told them how that I had been in prayer about what was going on in my body and how that the Lord had answered me and told me to tell them to remove the cysts, before they caused me problems." Now you can just imagine their response. They looked at me like I had just lost my mind. With a smile on their face, their reply was, No, and that they did not feel that there was a need for surgery, and that I would be alright and they would just continue drawing the fluid out. This went on for the space of two years. One morning early in the morning, while I was lying in my bed, I heard the voice of the Lord speaking to me, telling me to go to my doctor, that there was a problem with the cysts in my breasts. I immediately sat up and listened. He said, that since the cysts weren't removed when He told them to remove them, He was going to do the surgery Himself. I made the appointment to go in. I shared with them once again what the Spirit of the Lord had told me about there being a problem with the cysts in my breasts and because they were not taken out when He gave me the message for them to remove them, that He was going to do the surgery Himself. They just kind at smiled me again. I could tell they were in disbelief, and once again, said that they did not believe there was a problem, but they would check just to make sure, just to satisfy me. They withdrew the fluid as usual and went to the back. Sometime later they came back into room with a kind of somber look on their face. I already knew they had found something from what the Spirit of the Lord had already told me earlier. This time they did set me up for surgery, after finding cancer cells in the fluid drawn out of my breasts. I held onto faith! I went back to the Lord and told Him how that He said, that, No cancer would touch my body", and that it had! The Lord answered me back and said "He would take it". I asked the Lord, should I still take the surgery, He said, "Yes that He had to make a believer out of my doctor!" The day of the surgery, while I sitting at the admissions desk, I was praying within my spirit to the Lord as the receptionist was checking me in for the surgery. Feeling a little alone, for I was by myself and there was no one else to come with me at the time, I asked the Lord, was He still with me? Immediately I felt a warm gentle breeze just blow over my face, it felt like a soft caress as it just swirled all around my body, making my heart glad, and taking away the aloneness that I was starting to feel as I sitting there by myself. I knew it had to be the Spirit Lord assuring me that I was not alone and that He was right there with me. I looked around me just to make sure what I was receiving in my spirit truly was the Lord and I was not just reading something into something that was not so, I looked to see if there was a door open anywhere that a breeze could possibly come in, just to confirm it within myself it was not just my imagination. I even got up and walked a little ways down the hallway after I was checked in to see if I could detect the same breeze I felt as I was sitting and praying, asking the Lord if He was with me at the admissions desk. I was happy to see that there wasn't a door open anywhere, nor did I feel the breeze blow by me again. I was at peace. Oh how the Lord loves us!

Later on while they were getting me prepared for surgery, my doctor came and stood over me, watching as they prepared me and informing me that the surgery would not take long. Having my confidence boosted by the reassurance of the presence of the Lord, I told them that they were not going to find anything, because the Lord had already taken it. They went on to tell me, still not yet convinced about what I told them and with a kind of troubled look on their face, she said that they would see and that she knew what the test results had revealed. I didn't say anything else, not wanting to disturb them. I decided to let the Lord prove it Himself, knowing that what the Lord had spoken to me earlier, He was going to do, He had already done! Three and a half hours later they rolled me into the recovery room. When I opened my eyes, after coming out from under the anesthesia, there was my doctor once again, standing over me, they looked down at me and smiled and said, "Well, your God has given you a miracle." We could not find what we had found before, it was gone. They then went on to tell me how the surgery was supposed to last only an hour and a half, but because they could not find what they had found before, it was gone they kept looking two more hours! I smiled back at them and told, "I told you God said He took it, God said He would do the surgery Himself. They smiled once again with a look of amazement on their face and said that they still wanted me to come in two weeks from that day just to check and make sure and do another test. I said ok, and I did, all too happy to a witness of my Lord's miracle that He performed in my body and the keeping of His word of promise to me and still no cancer! Jesus said, No cancer would touch my body and He proved it before all those that did the surgery and all those that were over the findings of the test results and all those whom they shared the miracle with in the hospital that day. Later on while I was in the recovery room after the surgery, after I had fully recovered and was getting dressed to check out, one of the nurses that was in the recovery room, where I was taken after surgery came up to me and said, You're that woman that they found a cyst as big as the palm of her hand in one of my breasts, and three more cysts the size of golf balls in the other breast. A little embarrassed at the size of them, but thankful that they were gone, I listened as they went on to tell me how amazed everyone was at the size of the cysts and how that they didn't find what they were looking for. They then went on to tell me how that God had truly blessed me today! I shared with her what the Lord had told me during prayer so many years before, about no cancer touching my body and what He spoke into my spirit when they first found the cells and how I went before Him to remind Him of His promise to me, and how He did just what He said He was going to do! She happily agreed with me and said, Amen! I left the hospital that day victorious and having my confidence strengthened in the Lord all the more. I rejoiced in the word of the Lord, that which was spoken as well as that which is written! God honors His word, all of His word. That which He speaks as well as that which He has had written for all to receive! God performed spiritual surgery on me that day through His spoken word and promise! What He said to me and promised me so years before, and by faith was received, and believed He performed. Just like the centurion, who came to Christ to heal his servant who was at home sick in bed to the point of dying, trusting in the spoken word of Jesus Christ our Lord and Savior by faith, his servant was healed the very hour that Christ spoke it being far from where the servant was, so was I. This happened to me in the year 2005, I first prayed the prayer 25 years before in the year of 1980 when I was first saved, when I thought about how my father and how he had died. I asked the Lord to please not let me die of the same thing my father had died from, and the Lord promised me I wouldn't, and though it was far down the line in years, God remembered His word that He had spoke to me that day so long before during prayer when thinking about my father and though it had been a long time since I first made my request known, God answered me like it was yesterday! To God, be the Glory! I walked out of the hospital free from cancer, not because of the doctor, but because of the spiritual surgery that was performed on me through the spoken word of Jesus Christ before the scalpel could cut open my breasts, and with a testimony as to the greatness and the miracle working power of our Lord Jesus Christ and of the promise of the Father our God to share with others who might be going through the same similar trials, to take hold of faith and to believe in the Lord Jesus Christ for their selves, because God's hand is not shortened and His word still has power! To the unchanging God! Be all the Glory and the honor, Amen! I choose to take faith and trust in the word that was spoken into my spirit so long ago by the Holy Spirit, you can too! We today, are serving the same Lord and Savior as ones did back then, He hasn't changed, He is still all powerful, all knowing and all present at all times. He said He would never leave us nor forsake us and one thing I know is that God keeps His word!

For as the rain cometh down, and the snow from heaven, and returneth not thither, but watereth the earth, and maketh it bring forth and bud, that it may give seed to the sower, and bread to the eater:

So shall my word be that goeth forth out of my mouth: it shall accomplish that which I please, and it shall prosper in the thing whereto I sent it. - (Isaiah 55: 10, 11, KJV)

WITHOUT THE SMELL OF SMOKE

Shadrach, Meshach, and Abed-nego, answered and said to the king, O Nebuchadnezzar, we are not careful to answer thee in this matter.

If it be so, our God whom we serve is able to deliver us from the burning fiery furnace, and He is able to deliver us out of thine hand.

Then Nebuchadnezzar the king was astonied, and rose up in haste, and spake, and said unto his counselors, Did not we cast three men bound into the midst of the fire? They answered and said unto the king, True, O king.

He answered and said, Lo, I see four men loose, walking in the midst of the fire, and they have no hurt: and the form of the forth is like the Son of God.

Then Nebuchadnezzar came to the mouth of the burning fiery furnace, and said, Shadrach, Meshach, and Abed-nego, ye servants of the Most high God, come forth, and come hither. Then Shadrach, Meshach, and Abed-nego, came forth of the midst of the fire.

And the princes, governors, and captains, and the king's counselors, being gathered together, saw these men, upon whose bodies the fire had no power, nor was an hair of their head singed, neither were their coats changed, nor the smell of fire had passed on them. – (Daniel 3:16, 17, 24 – 27, KJV)

The three Hebrew young men, no doubt did not know how their circumstances were going to turn out, but their faith in God did not waver regardless. They had put their faith in God and trusted Him for their deliverance from the fiery furnace! Sometimes God allows things to happen to test us, to see if we will have the faith to trust in Him to deliver us or protect us. In these particular sets of scriptures we see the miraculous and supernatural protection of God. God allowed them to go into the fiery furnace, but He did not allow the fire to harm them nor did He let the smell of smoke cling to them or the fire to burn any part of them, not even the hairs of their heads. Jesus stood with them in the furnace and protected them from the fire because they trusted in Him. In **Psalm 27: 5, (KJV)**, we see that the Lord hides us in the secret place in Him, that place where the enemy and trouble cannot come. That place is His Spirit, which is well able to protect us in the midst of storm, trouble or harm. Now God does not always remove the danger or the trouble, but sometimes to prove to us that He is well able to protect us in the midst of the danger or trouble will deliver us none the less, He will deliver us from the affects of it. Now the Spirit of the Lord is that secret place where those who serve the Lord can find refuge, shelter and protection. When we pray or call upon the Lord Jesus to cover us in His blood, we are asking for the same protection that was given to the children of Israel when they spread the blood of the Lamb upon the door posts and the top of the door that covered and protected them from the death angel and from harm. Just as the blood of the lamb protected the children of Israel from harm in Egypt, so the shed blood of Jesus, the Lamb of God that was shed on Calvary for our sins, also protects us from hurt, harm and danger today when we call upon the Lord Jesus in prayer. The Lord hides us in the shadow of His wings, the covering of His spirit, through the shed blood of Jesus when we as His servants call upon Him. A life hidden in Christ can always find shelter from the storms of life natural or spiritual and peace in the time of trouble, when we depend upon Him and call upon His name. To God, be all the Glory!

"For in the time of trouble He shall hide me in His Pavilion: in the secret of His tabernacle shall He hide me; He shall set me up upon a rock." (Psalm 27: 5, KJV)

✦ Testimonies of the Heart:

One day while standing at the bus stop after work, waiting on the7:30 pm bus to come, a bad thunderstorm arose. I had brought my umbrella to work that day, but I still was hoping to be able to catch the bus home before the storm could start. When I first arrived at the transfer point to catch the second connecting bus to get home it was still nice and sunny out. It didn't look to be very many clouds in the sky at the time and I was glad for that. Thinking that I had made it before the storm could come, I was hoping that the next bus would get there on time before the weather had a chance to change. It was hot and humid out, and even though I was wearing lighter weight clothing, they were still work clothes and I could feel myself perspiring underneath them leaving me feeling very uncomfortable and anxious to get home and out of them into something cooler. Looking at my watch to see what time it was and then checking the bus schedule for when the time the bus was supposed to arrive, I saw that it was late, looking down the road, it was nowhere in sight. I then looked up the estimated time of the arrival of the next bus on my phone I noticed that it wasn't showing any arrival times. I knew that sometimes that the GPS on the buses was off which is what the eta used to give information concerning the arrival time of the next bus to the stop which you were standing at and this looked like it was going to be one of those times. I looked up at the sky as the scene was quickly changing from what was a sunny day with just a few clouds and to a grey looking sky. Dark clouds looked like they were blowing in quickly as the winds picked up and were starting to completely cover the sky! The wind also was becoming stronger as the minutes went by. I watched as the tops of the trees began to bend back and forth in the wind. I knew a storm was moving in fast! I looked around me to see if there was any place I could run to for shelter once the storm started, but there was nothing I could run up under to use as covering. I was completely in the open and exposed! The metal bus stop I had to stand by in order to be seen by the driver of the bus, stood right beside an electrical pole that had a generator on the top of it. There was no sidewalk, no light, nowhere to hid or run for cover, just grass and the road in front of me. There were a few pine trees with limbs growing and laying down to the ground. I couldn't stand there, trees draw lightning just as quickly as water. Just as quickly as the clouds covered the sky, the thunder and heat lightning began to cover the sky. In the midst of this there was streak lightning as well. It started pouring down rain in what seemed like literal buckets. The strong winds kept flipping my umbrella up and away from me, providing no cover at all. I had to keep straightening it out while getting completely soaked by the rain, and the worse part of it all, I was the only one at the bus stop. The bright sunny day disappeared quickly and was replaced by pitch dark blackness that covered the sky because of the storm clouds and the fact that it was now night! The clouds blocked out any light from the stars or the moon! Unfortunately where I was standing did not have a street light. The street light was around the corner on the other street. Where I was standing there was no light at all. I looked at my watch again by the light of my phone and checked the estimated time of arrival for the bus, still nothing was coming up. The storm was worsening and I began to pray to Jesus to cover me in His blood and to protect me from the lightning and the storm. I knew that if I was going to be helped, Jesus was the only one who could help me. The only light that shined on me in the midst of the blackness was coming from the few cars that passed me by as I stood at the bus stop under my umbrella in the storm. Soaking wet from my head to my toe, with nothing but big water puddles of rain in front of me in the road, wet grass and mud to stand in, a metal pole and a wooden electrical pole to stand with wet soaked trees behind me and electrical wires running all over my head, I had strike me printed all over my face! Excited now as the thunder and lightning seemed to grow stronger and stronger I could it feel the vibrations in the air every time it thundered loudly over head all around me! I stepped up my praying for the blood of Jesus to protect me. I started quoting every protective scripture I could think to remind myself of the Lord's protection of His saints, speaking them out loud to encourage myself. I had always been strongly afraid of thunder and lightning as a child which generally caused me to jump and want to run away to some place to hide myself from the noise and the lightning, but this time there was no place to go. This fear followed me into adulthood to my disliking and no matter how many times I tried to be brave, the Word of God and the Spirit of God are the only things that brought me comfort! There I was wearing all black standing in pitch blackness, with no light but the heat lightning that was lighting up everything all around me, along with that with streak as well a lightening flashing as well. Fewer and fewer cars were coming down the road to shine light on me. I told myself that if something were to happen to me, because of it being as dark, and as black as it was out, I might not be found till daylight. Fear was starting to grip me, but I kept on pleading the blood of Jesus to cover me and keep me safe because I knew that if anybody could Jesus could! I continued to speak the scriptures I knew that comforted me in times of trouble. The thunder was now booming directly over my head and the lightning flashed more and more frequent around me as I stood on the curb trying not to stand in the wet grass or the water flooded street in front of me, fearing that I might get struck quicker if I did, and the rain just poured all the harder!

Heat lightning and streak lightning lit up the sky all around me like momentary daylight as it lit up the sky and my surroundings. Soaked to the bone, and praying all I knew how for the Lord's protection and for the Lord to make the bus that was now extremely late to please come. All of a sudden the air lit up all around me like someone had flashed a bright yellowish, looking white light all around on me, the grass and all that was around me lit up in the flash of light. Suddenly it felt like thousands of worms were under my skin crawling up my body and the sides of my neck, and down into my arms and hands and fingers, and the sides of my neck and face as the electrical current was going through my body. I was looking at my hands and my fingers when it felt like whatever was crawling down my arms under my skin and into my hands on its way out through my fingers, started a burning sensation in the tips of my fingers! After the burning sensation there came a burning pain and a feeling of numbness in the tips of my fingers which seem to soon pass as it felt like whatever was going through my fingers left out of my body. After that, I felt the hairs on my neck and the sides of my face arms and body standing up all over me as if being pulled up by a magnet from the root!! After this suddenly, my neck stiffened and my head jerked over to the side and then my whole body immediately stiffened as if suddenly paralyzed, for a moment, I could not move. My neck felt like it was burning on the sides were the electrical current crawled under the skin. When I fully realized what had happened to me, I was in shock, because I was still alive! I knew it could only be Jesus! My head was feeling a little light, but my heart was still beating, thank you Jesus! Having heard of many suffering heart attacks and burning after being struck or shocked by lightning, I knew the Lord Jesus heard my prayer to cover me with His blood. Standing there somewhat dazed at what had just happened to me, I saw the head lights of the bus coming toward me. I flagged the bus down and jumped up on! Still a little dazed and light headed from what had just happened to me, I must have looked like I was dazed too. The bus driver looking at me at me asked me if I was alright. I told her that I had just got shocked by lightning and lived! Excited that I was still alive, I began to tell her what happened. I must have been looking a sight because she immediately asked me if I wanted her to call an ambulance or the paramedics! I said no, that I had prayed for the protection of the Lord by pleading the blood of Jesus to cover me, and He did and all I wanted was to go home! I told her about the flash of lightning, the crawling feeling under my skin, the hairs of my body standing up as if being pulled up and how that my body jerked and stiffened. The driver leaned over, sniffed me, surprised, and said, "I can't even smell any smoke on you". They asked me if my hair or clothes were burned anywhere, I told them I did not know. They got out of their seat and checked me out from top to bottom and upon leaning in closer they said, I don't see any hair burned on your head and there is no smell of smoke on you! It reminded me of the three Hebrew boys that had got put in the furnace and Jesus appeared in the furnace with them;

Then Nebuchadnezzar the king was astonied, and rose up in haste, and spake, and said unto his counselors, Did not we cast three men bound into the midst of the fire? They answered and said unto the king, True, O king.

He answered and said, Lo, I see four men loose, walking in the midst of the fire, and they have no hurt; and the form of the fourth is like the Son of God. – (Daniel 3:24 – 25, KJV)

They came out without being burned by the fire and without the smell of smoke on their clothes, all because they trusted in God to deliver them. I knew God had done the same miracle for me because I trusted in the power of the blood of Jesus when I asked the Lord Jesus to cover me in His spiritual blood! Jesus was my refuge! And His blood had protected me from the affects of the lightning! And now I am a living witness to His miraculous protection through the covering of His blood over me in the midst of the storm! Even though the lightning did shock me, but because of my faith in Jesus Christ and the protection through the covering of

His blood that was shed on Calvary, He kept me just like He did, Shadrach, Meshach, and Abed-nego in the fiery furnace. He allowed me to come out of this experience without the smell of smoke, without being burned or suffering from a heart attack or nerve damage as some do! How awesome is that?! He didn't stop the lightning, the rain nor the storm, just like He didn't put the fire out in the furnace for the three Hebrew boys, but He protected me in the midst of it all, just like He did those young men. All the effects in my body of what I had experienced in the storm that night when I was shocked by heat lightning went away as the evening passed, even the numbness and the burning that I was feeling in my fingers and the sides of my neck and face after I was shocked. It was as if it never happened, there is power in the blood of Jesus!! I couldn't wait until the next service night to share my story with the whole church. It to me was an experience I will never forget the rest of my life! To get shocked by lightning and live to tell the story, to me, it is the mercy of God, Hallelujah! This experience could have been my epitaph, but Jesus turned it into my victory! Truly, Jesus protected me that night standing at the bus stop in the midst of the storm surrounded by lightning! I believe in Jesus Christ and the power of His blood and I believe that because of this belief and faith in Him and His mercy and love for His people, Christ answered me and protected me. He allowed me to come out of the fire of the lightning without the smell of smoke, or being burned and still alive. Jesus stood with me in the midst of the lightning, just like He stood with the three Hebrew boys in the midst of the fiery furnace, glory to God! That night Jesus Christ became my secret hiding place, my tabernacle, my refuge and the blood of Jesus that was placed over me through the Spirit of the Lord protected me!

He that dwelleth in the secret place of the most High shall abide under the shadow of the Almighty

I will say of the LORD, He is my refuge and my fortress: my God; in Him will I trust. – (Psalm 91: 1, 2, KJV)

LITTLE BIRDS

When the LORD turned again the captivity
of Zion, we were like them that dream.

Then was our mouth filled with laughter,
and our tongue with singing: then said they
among the heathen, The LORD hath done
great things for them.

The LORD hath done great things for us;
whereof we are glad. – (Psalms 126:1-3, KJV)

In this particular Psalm, we see the Lord has given the
writer the joy of laughter and singing for something
that the Lord had done in his life. He says that his
mouth was filled with laughter and his tongue with
singing. Do you know that all creation rejoices in God
and what he does for them? Birds sing when they are
full and happy, marine animals frolic amongst the
waves of the ocean when there is no threat to them
near. Wolves lift their voices to howl and serenade at

the brightness of the light of the sun reflecting off the moon which allows them to see their way at night. Kittens and puppies jump and play in an environment where they do not have to fear. It has even been proven that house plants thrive in a happy environment and when you talk to them. My mother was someone with a green thumb. If it was a plant she could grow it. Often times I would catch her talking to her plants as she was taking care of them and it would seem as if they responded to her by just growing and filling out so beautifully. I asked her one day because as a child this was curious to me. She responded by telling me that plants grow better when you talk to them while you are taking care of them. At the time I thought this was silly, but later on in life after my mother passed, I found myself doing the same thing. I found that it had been proven by study and research that plants do respond to the vibrations in one's voice, and it is also said that they respond to the vibrations in music too. They even respond to how you touch them. It is said that though they do not have ears, plants can hear. Do you know that it has also been proven that plants make ultra sonic sounds when stressed from lack of water or rain, as well as when their stems are cut that humans cannot detect but insects can? Who would have thought that just being full of joy and laughter and singing would help produce life around you? God did, He gave all creation a voice of their own, whether it was through an audible voice or sounds created by sound vibrations. He even gave the stars in the heavens a voice, one that can be heard through the vibrating sounds coming from movement inside of the star. Sounds that travel through the universe that when recorded sounds like a musical instrument! The brighter the star the louder the sound that comes from it, how awesome is that! The brighter the star, kind of reminds you of how that the more of the light of Christ we let shine in our lives, the greater the praise we can give unto the Lord! God put His master plan of praise and worship in effect when He created the universe, the heavens and the earth and all that is therein. All of creation was made to praise the Lord and celebrate in the joy of the LORD together!

Where wast thou when I laid the foundations of the earth? declare, if thou hast understanding.

Who hath laid the measures thereof, if thou knowest? Or who hath stretched the line upon it?

Whereupon are the foundations thereof fastened? Or who laid the corner stone thereof;

When the morning stars sang together, and all the sons of God shouted for joy? – (Job 38: 4-7, KJV)

✦ Testimonies of the Heart:

One day when my children were in their teens, I was awakened to the sound of children laughing in my room. It was joyous playful laughter and it sounded like it was coming from the side of my bed! I immediately felt like in my spirit that these children whom I heard giggling and so full of joyous laughter had been standing at my bedside watching me while I slept. I opened my eyes and lifted up my head to see all who were in my room. I knew that it couldn't have been my children because my children were older and had deeper and more mature voices that fit their age. The voices of the children I heard at my bedside were much younger. They sounded like they may have been anywhere from three to maybe four or five years old, toddlers, they were light and airy. I jumped up and sat on the side of my bed having not seen who was doing the laughter, I thought that they may have ran out the room. But then I heard the laughter again coming from in front of me, again it felt like someone or some ones were in the room with me. Perplexed as to what was going on, and yet feeling the presence now in my spirit that what I was feeling and sensing was definitely spiritual, I saw what looked like little white lights, vague but visible none the least, appear and began to float away with the breeze as if being carried away with it and off into and through the window. As I watched this sight, the giggles and the laughter of the children soon turned into the sound of birds as this visible breeze which to me looked like wisps of air or clouds took the laughter of the children that had turned into the chirping of birds with it out the window. If I had not of experienced this for myself and seen what I seen and heard what I heard, I might not of believed it coming from someone else, but to God be the Glory it did happen and it happened to me. Still not knowing what to make of this I jumped to the window which was right at the head of my bed to the side, trying to catch sight of maybe children that might could have been playing outside my window as an possible solution as to why I was hearing what I was hearing, still not fully understanding what I had seen in my room. I thought that maybe they were in my yard and were possibly playing down below my window and the sound just travelled upward into my room since I had my window open, still not understanding how it was possible for their voices changed so audibly into the chirping of birds as well. As I looked out my window no one outside of my window, I was really surprised now. How could the sound of the joyous laughter I heard coming from the voices of children turn so strongly and audibly into the sound of birds chirping which then began to sound like the laughter of children mixing with the chirping of birds and then to completely sounding like birds chirping period was beyond me. If I had not been fully wake an experiencing this with my eyes open and listening to it with my ears as well having felt the physical presence of children in the room, and having seen the lights flowing with this very visible breeze in my room, I tell you, I might not of believed it myself, but it did happen just as I have described it to you. It was amazing!

I continued to look outside the window a few minutes more, still trying to see if there was the possibility of children playing outside my window, I was determined to try a find an explainable reason for what was happening. As I continued looking out my window, I heard the same chirping of the birds that came from the laughter of the children in my room, coming from the other side of my window screen below me. I shifted my gaze to the bottom of the window screen, there on the ledge of the window, sat little birds just chirping away to each other as if my presence in the window did not matter. I was amazed to say the least. How could this be? How could the human laughter of children come from birds chirping? And was the laughter that I heard coming from the voices of children actually be coming from these little birds perched on the ledge of my window? And why did I physically feel the presence of children in my room when I was lying down and when I sat up on the side of my bed? It actually felt like the physical presence of these children were standing over me watching me as I slept and when I sat up on the side of the bed they were still in my room. Visibly turning into what looked like little white lights that at times when they turned over and around in the breeze, resembled white flower petals being carried away by a wispy looking breeze! It was as if they had been watching me all along and when I woke up to the sound of their laughter, though I could not see the children themselves, I did see the little lights flowing in the breeze and was able to watch them as they flowed out the window as I heard the laughter turn into the sound of birds just joyously chirping away, and in their place were these little birds sitting on my window ledge. If I had not of witnessed it for myself, I might would have been inclined to think of it as being somewhat whimsical, but the fact of the matter is, I did witness it. While I was lying in the bed still trying to hold to the last few moments of sleep, when I first heard the giggles and playful laughter of the children, I saw in a picture in my mind, what looked like two little girls and two little boys standing at the side of my bed playfully giggling laughing while watching me sleep as if knowing to themselves that I did not know they were there. Have you ever thought it would be funny to sneak into someone's room while they were asleep as a child just to see the funny positions the individual ended up in the morning before they woke up? I did once to one of my sisters because she always ended up spread all over the bed and sometimes upside down, I thought it was funny at the time. When my son and my daughter were toddlers one Christmas season, I bought them both a pair of little Santa's elves pajamas. I thought they looked the cutest in them. One morning I woke up early and got my camera and took a picture of them sleeping in them, for memory's sake to have something to look back at and remember them when they were young. Well after the years went by and my children were older they no longer saw the joy in the pictures I took, to them they had become all but embarrassing and they would fuss when I brought them out, but to me, they were pure joy.

Thinking that my children had let them into the house and then, let them come into my room while I was sleeping. I thought that when I opened my eyes I would see who they were and catch them before they could run out. I was thinking to myself, that my children had some explaining to do for letting other children in the house while I was sleeping without my permission. All of this went through my head in a flash as I was lying in the bed listening to the sound of the children giggling and laughing at my bedside. It always amazes me when and how the Lord chooses to bless our day, to bring us into peace of mind knowing that He is with us and His joy is going before us to make our day lighter and brighter. That morning that I heard the children's laughter and the birds singing was such a joy for me.

This one event gave me so much encouragement and joy in the Lord that He would think of me that way to bless me to experience and see something as beautiful as that, sometimes I have no words to describe how glad I am to know that my Lord and Savior loves me like that. It was so personal and so uplifting it just brings to remembrance the sacrifice that He made on the cross for us to deliver us from having to experience an eternal separation from God the Father. I cannot think help but think about how blessed we are to have been given the opportunity to be saved and born again and experience all of God's goodness toward His people. We are blessed indeed and another thing, the Lord never said we would not have trials, but He did say, He would never leave us or forsake us and I have found that He is true to His word!

Peace I leave with you, my peace I give unto you: not as the world giveth, give I unto you. Let not your heart be troubled, neither let it be afraid – (John 14: 27, KJV)

THE ANGEL AND THE AIRPORT

Be not forgetful to entertain strangers: for thereby some have entertained angels unawares."– (Hebrews 13:2, KJV)

Many times in the word of God you read where many have at one time or another have entertained or encountered angels unawares that the Lord God sent to them to deliver a message, comfort, encourage or to do a work of the Lord. In the book of **Genesis** we see where Jacob while on his way back to the land of his fathers and his kindred, is met by a company of the angels of God;

And Jacob went on his way, and met him.

And when Jacob saw them, he said, This is God's host: and he called the name of that place Mahanaim. – (Genesis 32: 1, 2, KJV,) and is shown their encampment around him and his family and the company that followed him, named the place where the angels of God met him, Mahanaim, meaning two camps, Jacob's camp and the camp of God's angels who were with him to protect him from harm and his enemies. Jacob was returning back to the land where his brother Esau and his family lived. Knowing the bad blood that was between them and also knowing that he was defenseless and much concerned about his family, God sent an encampment of His angels to encamp around Jacob and also allowed him to see them to encourage him that he was with him and that he and all that he had would be protected from harm as well. After this reassurance of God's heavenly protection Jacob continued on to meet his brother. Sometimes when situations call for just a little more reassurance God sometimes will send an angel or angels to reinforce something where we are concerned or just to deliver a word of encouragement on our behalf. Whenever or however God chooses to do such a thing it is up to Him, but I can guarantee you whenever He does this it is always welcome and much needed, to God be the Glory!

→ Testimonies of the Heart:

In the year 2010, I was working at the airport. I was working in the store alone as my store was very small. Thankful that I was the only one working in the store, I would often pray and sing quietly while working around the store, this made me happy, for at the time I was going through some trying times with an injury I had sustained, and praying and singing praises unto God helped to take my mind off of things and focus on the goodness of the Lord. The store faced the main checkpoint of the airport and often there were crowded lines outside my door going through the check point and many people standing and walking to and fro in front of the store. My store sold a lot of souvenir items and such for the different travelers and guests to pick up while waiting or walking around the airport. This one day I had been praying deeply about some things that concerned me and just having a talk with the Lord and just singing to myself while the store was empty and there were no customers coming in. I was at the counter taking some things out of the boxes setting them on the counter to go out on the shelves. Out of the corner of my eye, I saw a kind of tall blonde haired woman, who looked to be in her thirties or forties dressed in a pretty light blue suite come walking in the store. I always have been quick to notice people because of being trained to keep an eye out for customers and being able to anticipate their needs in order to make a suggestion pertaining to what they might be looking to buy. Seeing that she was quite, and didn't seem to mind my singing, I continued to sing quietly to myself. My singing the praises of the Lord has always comforted me when I am going through stuff. Finally, she spoke as she came and stood at the right side of the counter. She told me I had a beautiful voice. I was surprised, but very appreciative of the compliment, because everybody when they come around you are not appreciative of you singing about the Lord around them, even if you are singing low. I knew I was in the presence of someone who loved the Lord Jesus, it was refreshing. I knew I could let my guard down and enjoy the spirit of the Lord. I cannot remember all our conversation from that point, other than it involved talking about the goodness of the Lord and that I was doing most of the talking. I felt like this was someone I could talk too without feeling hindered. It was relieving. She listened patiently as I talked, as if receiving every word. It felt good to be able to talk about the Lord without feeling that you had to walk on eggshells or offending somebody who did not understand what you were talking about. She just smiled all the while I was talking and this just spurred me on even more to share my heart for Jesus with her. Finally, when I had shared all I could think of at that point, not trying to talk her death, or seemingly over talkative, I quieted down. She just looked at me and smiled and said to me just as confirmative as if it had already been done or accomplished, "I will see you again in heaven." Not one day in heaven as most Christians often like to say when salutations are being given in order to encourage one another, but just plainly, "I will see you again in heaven." As I said, I am quick to pick up on people, and right off the bat, I recognized that this was no ordinary salutation. I looked at her as she quickly turned to walk out the store after making the comment. I stood there for a minute pondering her confirmative point about seeing me again in heaven and she said it and just walked out the store. I quickly came out from behind the counter and kind of ran to the doorway to see where was going. From where the store was positioned, I could see everything in the immediate area. She was nowhere to be found. I took a chance and stepped out the store and quickly went to the corner of the store to see if she had gone around the store. I knew that because of the crowd she could not have gotten far. Nothing! As tall as she was and as light as her suit an hair was I knew she would be easy to spot, again, nothing. This happened not too long after a minister had come into my store and was standing in the corner just looking. The Holy Spirit spoke to me and told me he was a minister and I was to talk to him. I prayed first for the Lord to put the words in my mouth to say unto him and to please reveal him to me. When He did, I walked over and asked him if he would mind if I spoke a word into his spirit what the Lord had given me about him? He told me that he didn't mind. The Lord showed me how that enemy was trying to get him to lay down his ministry by constantly attacking who he was in Christ and the work that the Lord had given him to do through others, to the point of accusing him of not even being a minister and it was becoming very grievous to him and causing him to question if he had been called by the Lord to minister. The attack upon him centered around a word spoken unto him in the spirit about moving and taking over pastor of another church out of state and was confirmed when he actually got the offer, those that were close unto him and around him began to immediately attack the word that was given him and his calling in ministry by the Holy Spirit and were even more upset that God manifested the offer. Not wanting to move they began to discourage his going there by constantly attacking him verbally trying to intimidate him into not going. As the Holy Spirit was giving me what to say, tears began to well up in his eyes. I shared with him what the Holy Spirit was saying to me how that he had been called by God to minister and that he was a Pastor from the head to his toe and, yes it was His will for him to go and not to worry that God was going to make sure that whom he was concerned about being with him was going to be with him, despite their trying to intimidate him and attacking his calling. He smiled at me, and told me how that he had no intentions of stopping in my store but that as he was passing by, the Lord told him to come in my store. He went on further to say that he didn't even know why he stopped here, that's why he was just standing in the corner. I told him that the Lord Jesus Christ had a divine intervention set up for him and it was for him to hear what the Lord had to say. He gave me a big hug and thanked me for letting the Lord use me to say what I said unto him. I told him, I may not know you, but God knows all about us and what we need to hear when we need to hear it and blesses us accordingly by putting somebody in our path to be a witness unto Him. For this I thank the Lord for being able to use me that day to be of a confirming word about someone's walk with the Lord. Truly the Lord is faithful to encourage and to acknowledge our praise of Him for being in and at the head of our lives. Just like that day he sent the angel to the store to encourage me and make my heart glad at the words that were spoken to me, and for this, and much, much more I will always be thankful and give Him the praise!

REFLECTIONS

I've never considered myself an author or a writer, even though I was always writing. Sometimes just to put into my remembrance things the Holy Spirit would reveal unto me while studying the word of God, or thoughts that would come to me concerning what was revealed. All this I just looked at it as Bible study and words to help me to remember what I had learned. Never in my life did I think that I would be writing books on what the Lord has revealed to me and what He has done for me, but here again, God's plans are not always our plans. Sometimes the Holy Ghost has to bring us into the plans of God for our life. Moses for example had to be placed on the backside of the dessert before God could bring him into understanding what He had called and wanted him to do. David, even though the oil of anointing was poured on his head as a young man, some say he was only 17 at the time to be Israel's next King, ended up running for his life for many years before He could actually assume the position, when God showed Joseph in a dream of his father, mother and brothers bowing down to him, I do not believe that for one moment he knew that God was going to make him a ruler in Egypt, second only to Pharoah, not only having his brethren bowing down but all of Egypt and many others from other nations who came to Egypt seeking grain. Sometimes God's plans are for later in our lives when we have matured spiritually to a place and point whereas He can trust us with certain assignments to do them and accomplish His will in and through our lives for the blessing and encouragement of others, and there are even more powerful testimonies that I have shared in the first book that the Holy Spirit gave me to write, called, "Visions, What The Preacher Saw". Christ has done so many things in my life and He is still doing great and mighty, and wondrous things in my life, that if I were to try a write about them all it would make this book too long to be read. Instead I wanted to just give a glimpse of what a Mighty God and loving Savior we serve and what a powerful anointing the Holy Spirit carries that we have dwelling with us, and also to let you know that all of heaven is with us and we are never alone. To know that there is nothing impossible for God to do. He is almighty – omnipotent, all knowing – omniscient, all present at all times – omnipresent, and there is nothing to hard for Him to do! God bless you and I hoped you enjoyed this look into some of the times in my life when My Lord and Savior just impressed upon me His great loving care and His enduring love for His children. Truly God in Christ is a miracle worker, a loving Father, and a true friend. He is all that and more! Yes, He is and will forever be, Day of Sunshine!

ABOUT THE AUTHOR

Dianne Chatman was called to the ministry in the year 1980 having been Born again and filled with the precious Holy Ghost have had witnessed and experienced many a miracle, signs and wonders in her life and her walk with Christ. Gifted by the Holy Spirit with dreams and visions, she has always had a heart for the people to share the word of God and the many signs and wonders of God. Her testimony of what God has done in her life alone has inspired all who have heard her speak. To know that we don't just serve a God of the possible, but a God of the impossible as well!

Printed in the United States
By Bookmasters